QUILTING FOR
CHRISTMAS

Created for Leisure Arts by House of White Birches

QUILTING FOR CHRISTMAS

LEISURE ARTS STAFF

Vice President and Editor-in-Chief **Susan White Sullivan**
Quilt Publications Director **Cheryl Johnson**
Special Projects Director **Susan Frantz Wiles**
Senior Prepress Director **Mark Hawkins**
Art Publications Director **Rhonda Shelby**
Imaging Technician **Stephanie Johnson**
Prepress Technician **Janie Marie Wright**
Publishing Systems Administrator **Becky Riddle**
Mac Information Technology Specialist **Robert Young**

President and Chief Executive Officer **Rick Barton**
Vice President of Sales **Mike Behar**
Director of Finance and Administration **Laticia Mull Dittrich**
National Sales Director **Martha Adams**
Creative Services **Chaska Lucas**
Information Technology Director **Hermine Linz**
Controller **Francis Caple**
Vice President, Operations **Jim Dittrich**
Retail Customer Service Manager **Stan Raynor**
Print Production Manager **Fred F. Pruss**

Library of Congress Control Number: 2011934170

ISBN-13/EAN: 978-1-60900-360-9

10 9 8 7 6 5 4 3 2 1

HOUSE OF WHITE BIRCHES STAFF

Editor **Jeanne Stauffer**
Creative Director **Brad Snow**
Publishing Services Director **Brenda Gallmeyer**
Editorial Assistant **Stephanie Franklin**
Assistant Art Director **Nick Pierce**
Copy Supervisor **Deborah Morgan**
Copy Editors **Emily Carter, Mary O'Donnell**
Technical Proofreader **Angie Buckles**
Production Artist Supervisor **Erin Augsburger**
Graphic Artist **Jessi Butler**
Production Assistants **Marj Morgan, Judy Neuenschwander**
Technical Artist **Debera Kuntz**
Photography Supervisor **Tammy Christian**
Photography **Scott Campbell, Matthew Owen**
Photo Stylists **Tammy Liechty, Tammy Steiner**

Copyright © 2012 by Leisure Arts, Inc., 5701 Ranch Drive, Little Rock, AR 72223. All rights reserved. This publication is protected under federal copyright laws. Reproduction or distribution of this publication or any other Leisure Arts publication, including publications which are out of print, is prohibited unless specifically authorized. This includes, but is not limited to, any form of reproduction or distribution on or through the Internet, including posting, scanning, or email transmission.

We have made every effort to ensure that these instructions are accurate and complete. We cannot, however, be responsible for human error, typographical mistakes, or variations in individual work.

Introduction

This book is packed full of projects to keep your home looking festive all winter long. Patterns are included for mini quilts, runners, wall quilts, bed quilts and more!

If you like paper piecing, you will love making Big Things Come in Small Packages, page 6. These are perfect for gift giving and can be stitched in a day! Celtic Christmas Table Runner on page 20 is another fun paper-piecing pattern to try. The unique design is sure to be a conversation piece at dinner. You will also love using fusible web to create the Ornament Wall Hanging pattern on page 52.

If patchwork quilting is more your style, then Redesign Nine Quilt & Runner on page 83 is a must. The pattern is great when made up in holiday colors, but can also be made in almost any other color combination, making it great for every season! Christmas Counterchange on page 63 is another great patchwork design, and it can easily be made by a beginner.

Now is the time to dig out all of those holiday fabrics you have been itching to use all year! With all of the wonderful projects in this book, it's never too early to get started!

TABLE OF CONTENTS

Big Things Come in Small Packages

DESIGN BY CONNIE KAUFFMAN

Big things do come in small packages, and these quilted treasures are no exception. Stitch them ahead of time to give as gifts.

Pineapple
Placement Diagram 6" x 6"

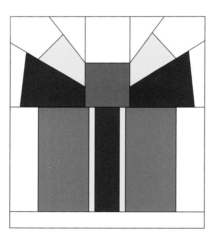

Present
Placement Diagram 6" x 6¾"

Project Specifications

Skill Level: Beginner
Quilt Sizes: 6" x 6" and 6" x 6¾"

Materials

- Dark, light and medium green scraps
- Yellow solid, tonal and print scraps
- Red solid, tonal and print scraps
- ¼ yard red mottled
- ¼ yard green tonal
- ¼ yard white tonal
- Backing 2 (9") squares
- Batting 2 (9") squares
- Neutral-color all-purpose thread
- Invisible thread for quilting
- Paper
- 2 hanging stands
- Basic sewing tools and supplies

Cutting

1. Cut green, yellow and red scraps as directed in instructions for paper piecing.

2. From red mottled and green tonal, cut one each 1¼" x 36" binding strip and 2½" x 6½" hanging sleeve.

3. Cut white tonal as directed in instructions for paper piecing.

Completing the Pineapple Project

1. Prepare one copy of the Pineapple Paper-Piecing pattern.

2. Cut one 13/8" square white tonal for piece 1.

3. Cut four 2¼" dark green scrap squares; cut each square in half on one diagonal to make triangles for pieces 50–53. Discard one triangle of each fabric.

4. Cut a variety of dark and light green scraps into 1"-wide strips.

5. Set machine stitch length to 15 stitches per inch or 1.5. Pin piece 1 right side up in the No. 1 position on the unmarked side of the paper.

6. Place a light green strip right sides together with piece 1; stitch on the 1–2 line on the marked side of the paper as shown in Figure 1. Press the strip to the right side to cover area 2 and extend ¼" into areas 6, 9 and 10. Trim excess length.

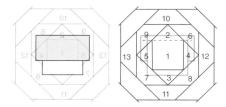

Figure 1

7. Repeat step 6 with all pieces in numerical order, alternating light and dark green strips, referring to the pattern for color placement. Add a dark green triangle to each outer corner; press all pieces to the right side after stitching.

8. When stitching is complete, trim outside edges along solid line and remove paper.

9. Layer and quilt referring to Finishing Your Quilt on page 96.

10. Fold one long edge of the green binding strip ¼" to the wrong side; press.

11. With right sides together and raw edges even, stitch the binding strip around all sides of the quilted top, mitering corners and overlapping at the beginning and end.

12. Press the binding to the right side and over to the back side; hand-stitch in place to finish.

Completing the Present Project

1. Prepare two copies of each Present Paper-Piecing pattern, including number and cutting information. Cut one pattern apart on solid lines to make separate templates for each shape.

2. Place a paper shape printed side up on the wrong side of fabric scraps and trace; cut out each shape, adding ½" all around when cutting. ***Note:*** *You don't have to be exact when cutting these pieces; they are just guides to make sure your pieces are large enough to cover the spaces on the paper-piecing pattern.*

3. Set machine stitch length to 15 stitches per inch or 1.5.

4. For each pattern, pin fabric piece 1 right side up in the No. 1 position on the unmarked side of the uncut paper pattern.

5. Place fabric piece 2 right sides together with fabric piece 1; stitch on the 1-2 line on the marked side of the paper as shown in Figure 2. Press piece 2 to the right side.

Figure 2

6. Repeat step 5 with all pieces in numerical order to complete each paper-pieced section; press all pieces to the right side after stitching.

7. Trim each pieced section on the outside solid line.

8. Join the pieced sections referring to Figure 3 to complete the Present block top.

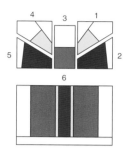

Figure 3

9. Layer and quilt referring to Finishing Your Quilt on page 96.

10. Fold one long edge of the red binding strip ¼" to the wrong side; press.

11. With right sides together and raw edges even, stitch the binding strip around all sides of the quilted top, mitering corners and overlapping at the beginning and end.

12. Press the binding to the right side and over to the back side; hand-stitch in place to finish.

Adding Hanging Sleeves

1. Fold in each end of one sleeve strip ¼" and press; fold under ¼" again and stitch to hem.

2. Fold the strip in half along length with right sides together; stitch to make a tube.

3. Turn right side out and press with seam at one side.

4. Repeat steps 1–3 to make a green hanging sleeve.

5. Hand-stitch a hanging sleeve to the back side of each quilted project for hanging. △

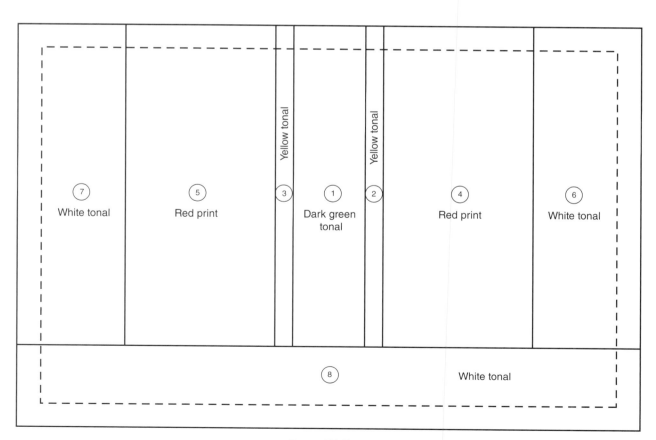

Present Pattern
Make 2 copies

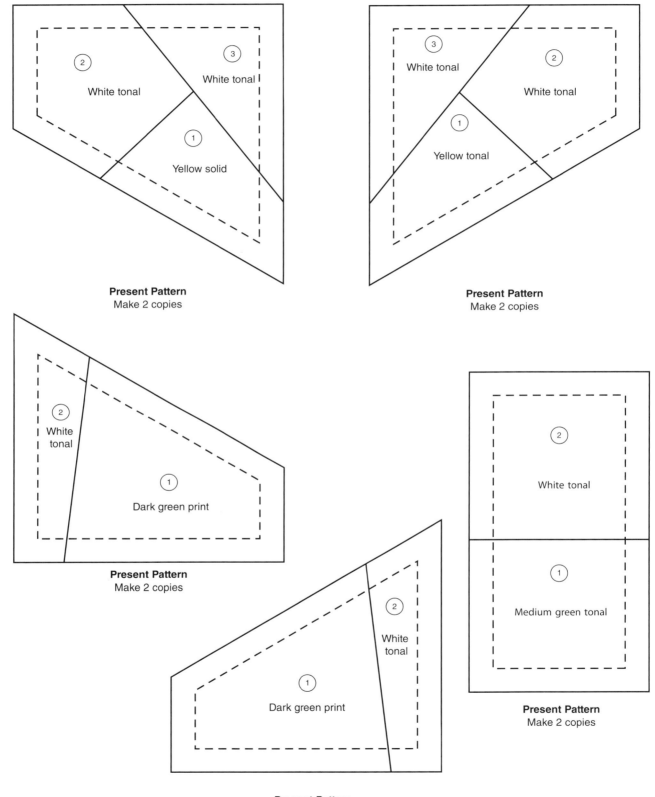

Present Pattern
Make 2 copies

Present Pattern
Make 2 copies

Present Pattern
Make 2 copies

Present Pattern
Make 2 copies

Present Pattern
Make 2 copies

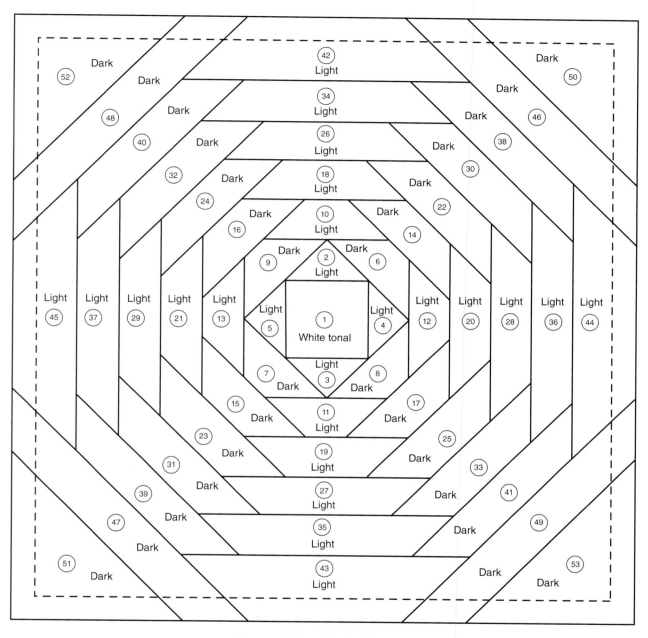

Pineapple Paper-Piecing Pattern
Make 1 copy

Poinsettia Table Runner

DESIGN BY BRENDABARB DESIGNS

BY BRENDA CONNELLY AND BARBARA MILLER

A simple pieced runner base is elegant with just a bit of appliqué in the center.

Project Specifications

Skill Level: Beginner
Runner Size: 40" x 18", without prairie points

Materials

- 4" square gold scrap
- 5 (6" x 12") red scraps from very dark burgundy to light red-orange
- 2 (6" x 12") scraps contrasting greens
- 1½" x 12" J strip green tonal
- 5/8 yard white tonal
- ¾ yard gold metallic tonal
- Backing 43" x 21"
- Batting 43" x 21"
- Neutral-color all-purpose thread
- Invisible thread
- Quilting thread
- ½ yard 12"-wide lightweight double-stick fusible web
- ½ yard fabric stabilizer
- Brown, black and dark green permanent fabric markers
- Appliqué pressing sheet
- Basic sewing tools and supplies

Cutting

1. Cut one 12½" by fabric width strip white tonal; subcut into one 12½" A square and four 2½" x 18½" F strips.

2. Cut one 1½" by fabric width C strip white tonal.

3. Cut one 2" by fabric width strip white tonal; subcut strip into eight 4½" G pieces.

4. Cut one 1½" by fabric width B strip gold metallic tonal.

5. Cut two 2½" by fabric width strips gold metallic tonal; subcut strips into two 14½" D strips and two 18½" E strips.

6. Cut two 2" by fabric width strips gold metallic tonal; subcut strip into 12 (4½") H pieces.

7. Cut one 2" by fabric width I strip gold metallic tonal; subcut into two 12" I pieces.

8. Cut one 3½" by fabric width strip gold metallic tonal; subcut strip into two 18½" K strips.

9. Cut two 2½" by fabric width strips gold metallic tonal; subcut strips into 18 (2½") L squares.

Completing the Pieced Top

1. Sew the B strip to the C strip with right sides together along length to make a B-C strip set; press seams toward B.

2. Subcut the B-C strip set into 26 (1½") B-C units as shown in Figure 1.

Figure 1

3. Join six B-C units end to end to make a B-C strip as shown in Figure 2; press seams in one direction. Repeat to make two B-C strips.

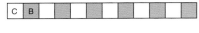

Figure 2

4. Sew a B-C strip to opposite sides of A as shown in Figure 3; press seams toward A.

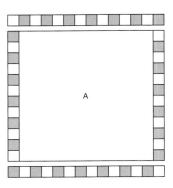

Figure 3

5. Join seven B-C units end to end to make a longer B-C strip; press seams in one direction. Repeat to make two longer B-C strips.

6. Sew the longer B-C strips to the top and bottom of A, again referring to Figure 3; press seams toward A.

7. Referring to the Placement Diagram, sew D to opposite sides and E to the top and bottom of the A-B-C unit to complete the pieced center; press seams toward D and E.

8. Sew the J strip between the two I strips with right sides together along length; press seams toward J.

9. Subcut the I-J strip set into six 1½" I-J units as shown in Figure 4.

Figure 4

10. Sew H to opposite sides of an I-J unit to complete an H-I-J unit as shown in Figure 5; press seams toward H pieces. Repeat to make six H-I-J units.

Figure 5

11. Join three H-I-J units with four G pieces to make a pieced row as shown in Figure 6; press seams away from G. Repeat to make two pieced rows.

Figure 6

12. Sew an F strip to opposite sides of each pieced row; add K to one side to complete an end unit as shown in Figure 7; press seams toward F and K.

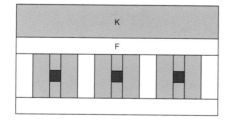

Figure 7

13. Referring to the Placement Diagram, sew an end unit to the center unit to complete the pieced top; press seams toward the center unit.

Completing the Appliqué

1. Trace the appliqué shapes onto the paper side of the fusible web as directed on patterns; cut out shapes, leaving a margin around each one.

2. Fuse shapes to the wrong side of fabrics as directed on patterns for color; cut out shapes on traced lines. Remove paper backing.

3. Referring to the instructions with the appliqué pressing sheet and using the full-size motifs given, create one large and two small poinsettia motifs, layering pieces in numerical order.

4. Arrange the motifs with leaves on the pieced center referring to the Placement Diagram and project photo for positioning; when satisfied with placement, fuse shapes in place.

5. Cut one 16" x 16" square fabric stabilizer; pin to the wrong side of the center A area of the pieced top.

6. Using invisible thread, machine buttonhole-stitch around each fused shape; remove fabric stabilizer.

7. Add vines, leaf and flower-center details as marked on pattern using permanent fabric markers in appropriate colors to complete the runner top.

Completing the Runner

1. Fold each L square in half and in half again to create a prairie point triangle as shown in Figure 8.

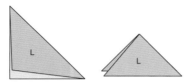

Figure 8

2. Pin one L prairie point in the center and at each end of each K strip on the runner ends as shown in Figure 9.

Figure 9

3. Arrange and pin three more L prairie points between the center and each end as shown in Figure 10, overlapping prairie points as necessary to fit edge;

when satisfied with positioning, machine-baste in place 1/8" from edge.

Figure 10

4. Place backing piece right side up on batting; place completed top right sides together with backing; pin edges.

5. Trim backing and batting even with the pieced top.

6. Sew all around, leaving a 6" opening along one side; clip inner corners. Trim batting close to stitching.

7. Turn right side out through opening; press edges flat.

8. Turn opening edges to the inside; hand-stitch opening closed.

9. Quilt as desired by hand or machine to finish. △

Poinsettia Table Runner
Placement Diagram 40" x 18", without prairie points

Small Poinsettia Motif A
Cut 1 each petal red scraps
Cut 1 each leaf green scrap
Cut 1 center gold scrap

Small Poinsettia Motif B
Cut 1 each petal red scraps
Cut 1 each leaf green scrap
Cut 1 center gold scrap

Large Poinsettia Motif
Cut 1 each petal red scraps
Cut 1 leaf green scrap
Cut 1 center gold scrap

Top

Celtic Christmas Table Runner

DESIGN BY BARBARA CLAYTON

Interwoven pieces create the Celtic design in the blocks of this holiday runner.

Project Specifications

Skill Level: Intermediate
Runner Size: 34½" x 14½"
Block Size: 7" x 7"
Number of Blocks: 3

Materials

- 1/8 yard red solid
- 1/8 yard dark green tonal 1
- ¼ yard Kelly green mottled
- 1/3 yard dark green tonal 2
- 3/8 yard red mottled
- ½ yard cream tonal
- Backing 39" x 19"
- Batting 39" x 19"
- All-purpose thread to match fabrics
- Quilting thread
- Clear nylon monofilament
- 1/8 yard fusible web
- Freezer paper
- Water-erasable marker or pencil
- Water-soluble glue stick
- Basic sewing tools and supplies

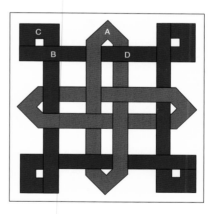

Celtic Christmas
7" x 7" Block
Make 3

Cutting

1. Cut three 7½" E squares cream tonal.

2. Cut three 2¼" by fabric width strips cream tonal for binding.

3. Cut one 11¼" square red mottled; cut the square on both diagonals to make four F triangles.

4. Cut two 57/8" squares red mottled; cut each square in half on one diagonal to make four G triangles.

5. Cut two 1¼" x 30½" H strips and two 1¼" x 12" I strips dark green tonal 2.

6. Cut two 2" x 32" J strips and two 2" x 15" K strips Kelly green mottled.

Preparing the Appliqué Pieces

1. Trace A–D patterns onto freezer paper as indicated on each piece.

2. Press the waxy side of the freezer paper onto the wrong side of fabrics as directed on patterns for color and number to cut.

3. Cut out fabric shapes, leaving ¼" beyond the edges of the freezer paper all around.

4. Clip corners and indentations almost to the paper pattern.

5. Glue seam allowance to the freezer paper all the way around the edges of the A pieces; cut through the glued A pieces where indicated on pattern to allow for tucking under other pattern pieces.

6. Glue seam allowances under all around on remaining pieces, leaving ¼" unglued where indicated by dashed lines on each piece.

7. Prepare template for the yo-yo circle; cut as directed.

8. Turn one yo-yo circle edge under 1/8"; using a double thread and a running stitch, sew around folded edge referring to Figure 1. Pull the thread to gather the fabric tightly and knot to secure. Flatten the gathered circle to form a yo-yo berry. Repeat to make 16 yo-yo berries.

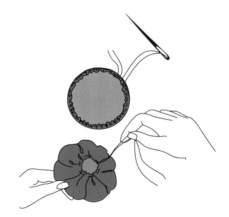

Figure 1

9. Trace the holly leaf pattern onto the paper side of the fusible web as directed on pattern for number to cut; cut out shapes, leaving a margin around each one.

10. Fuse shapes to the wrong side of the dark green tonal 1; cut out shapes on marked lines. Remove paper backing.

Completing the Blocks

1. Fold each E square and crease to mark the vertical, horizontal and diagonal centers.

2. Transfer the full-size block drawing given to each E square using a water-erasable marker or pencil.

3. Arrange, pin and baste pieces to each E square in numerical order as marked on the full-size pattern, tucking ends under other pieces as marked on pattern.

4. Using clear nylon monofilament and a narrow machine blind-hemstitch, stitch around all the edges of each piece.

5. Wet the back side of each block, cut a slit behind each appliqué piece and remove the freezer paper. Let dry; lightly press each block.

Completing the Quilt

1. Join the blocks with the F and G triangles in diagonal rows as shown in Figure 2; press seams toward F and G.

Figure 2

2. Join the diagonal rows to complete the pieced center; press seams in one direction.

3. Arrange and fuse holly leaves on the F and G triangles referring to the Placement Diagram for positioning.

4. Sew H strips to opposite long sides and I strips to the short ends of the pieced center; press seams toward H and I strips.

5. Sew J strips to opposite long sides and K strips to the short ends of the pieced center; press seams toward J and K strips to complete the pieced top.

6. Arrange and pin yo-yo berries in place on holly leaves referring to the Placement Diagram.

7. Layer, quilt and bind referring to Finishing Your Quilt on page 96, using thread to match fabrics and a machine blind-hemstitch to stitch around holly leaves and yo-yo berries during the quilting process. △

Holly Leaf
Cut 12 dark
green tonal 1

Yo-Yo Circle
Cut 16 red solid

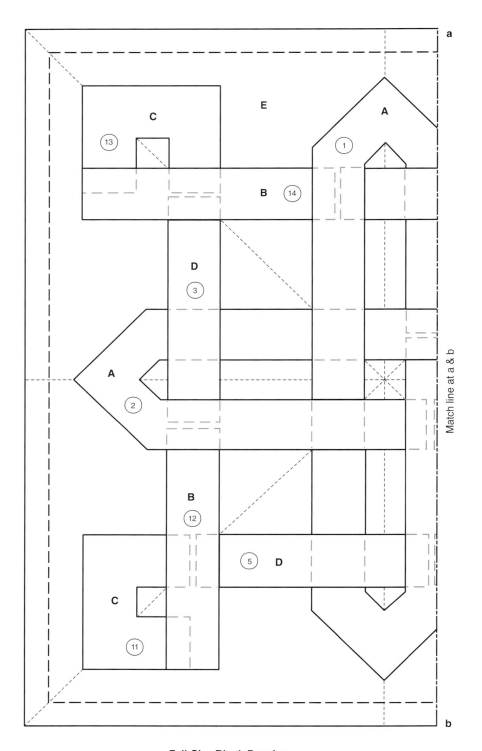

Match line at a & b

Full-Size Block Drawing
Arrange pieces, tucking under as marked.

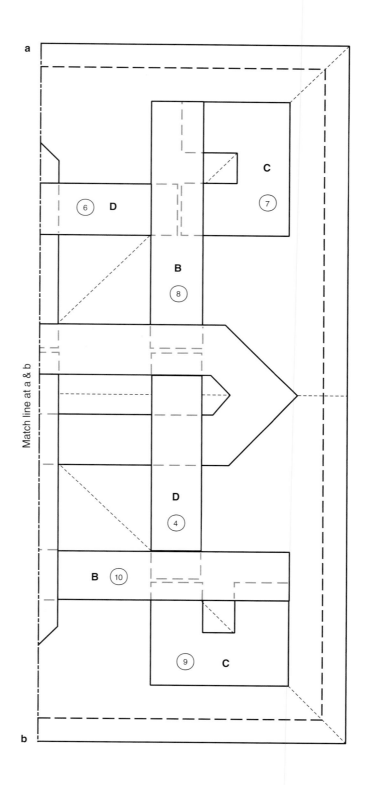

Celtic Christmas Runner
Placement Diagram 34¹/₂" x 14¹/₂"

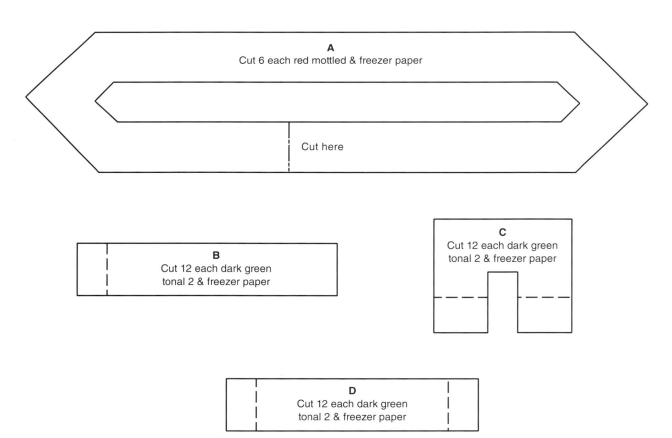

A
Cut 6 each red mottled & freezer paper

Cut here

B
Cut 12 each dark green
tonal 2 & freezer paper

C
Cut 12 each dark green
tonal 2 & freezer paper

D
Cut 12 each dark green
tonal 2 & freezer paper

Star Bright Table Set

DESIGN BY JODI GRENZNER OF QUILTER'S ROOST

A matching runner and set of four place mats dress up any table at Christmastime.

Project Specifications

Skill Level: Beginner
Runner Size: 54" x 24"
Place Mat Size: 19" x 13½"
Block Size: 6" x 6"
Number of Blocks: 30

Materials

- Scraps green prints and brown check
- ½ yard gold star print
- 2/3 yard gold tonal
- ¾ yard gold stripe
- 7/8 yard green stripe
- 1¾ yards dark red print
- Backing 60" x 30"
- Batting 60" x 30" and 4 (25" x 19") pieces
- All-purpose thread to match fabrics
- Quilting thread
- ½ yard 18"-wide fusible web
- ½ yard fabric stabilizer
- Basic sewing tools and supplies

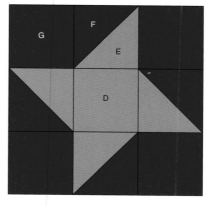

Star
6" x 6" Block
Make 30

Cutting

1. Cut one 11" x 41" A rectangle from gold star print.

2. Cut two 2½" by fabric width strips from gold tonal; subcut into 30 (2½") D squares.

3. Cut five 27/8" by fabric width strips gold tonal; subcut into 60 (27/8") E squares.

4. Cut eight 2½" by fabric width strips from gold stripe for placemat binding.

5. Cut two 1¼" x 41" B rectangle from green stripe.

6. Cut seven 1¼" by width of fabric strips from green stripe; subcut into 10 (1¼" x 12½") C stripes and eight 1¼" x 19½" I strips.

7. Cut five 2¼" by fabric width strips from green stripe for runner binding.

8. Cut five 27/8" by fabric width strips from dark red print; subcut into 60 (27/8") F squares.

9. Cut eight 2½" by fabric width strips from dark red print; subcut into 120 (2½") G squares.

10. Cut two 12" by width of fabric strips from dark red print; subcut into four 12" x 12½" H rectangles.

Completing the Blocks

1. Draw a diagonal line from corner to corner on the wrong side of each E square.

2. Place an E square right sides together with an F square; stitch ¼" on each side of the marked line as shown in Figure 1.

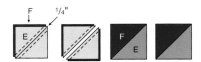

Figure 1

3. Cut apart on the marked line to make two E-F units, again referring to Figure 1; press seams toward F.

4. Repeat steps 2 and 3 to complete 120 E-F units.

5. To complete one Star block, sew an E-F unit to opposite sides of D to complete the center row as shown in Figure 2; press seams toward D.

Figure 2

6. Sew G to opposite sides of a D-E unit to make the top row, again referring to Figure 2; press seams toward G. Repeat to make the bottom row.

7. Sew the top and bottom rows to the center row referring to the block drawing to complete one Star block; press seams toward the center row.

8. Repeat steps 5–7 to complete 30 Star blocks, pressing seams in half the blocks toward the center row and half the seams away from the center row.

Completing the Runner

1. Trace tree shapes onto the paper side of the fusible web as directed on pattern for number to cut; cut out shapes, leaving a margin around each one.

2. Fuse shapes to the wrong side of fabrics as directed on patterns; cut out shapes on traced lines. Remove paper backing.

3. Arrange and fuse the tree shapes to A as shown in Figure 3, overlapping shapes as marked on patterns.

Figure 3

4. Cut two 8" x 14" pieces fabric stabilizer; pin one piece to the wrong side of each fused area.

5. Using thread to match fabrics, stitch a narrow machine zigzag stitch around each fused shape.

6. Sew B strips to opposite long sides and C strips to the short ends of the appliquéd A center; press seams toward B and C strips.

7. Join seven Star blocks to make a block strip, alternating seam pressing; press seams in one direction. Repeat to make two block strips.

8. Sew a block strip to opposite long sides of the appliquéd A center; press seams toward B strips.

9. Join four Star blocks to make an end strip, alternating seam pressing; press seams in one direction. Repeat to make two end strips.

10. Sew an end strip to opposite short ends of the appliquéd A center to complete the runner top; press seams toward C strips.

11. Layer, quilt and bind referring to Finishing Your Quilt on page 96.

Completing the Place Mats

1. To complete one place mat, join two Star blocks with alternating seam allowances; press seams in one direction.

2. Sew the block strip to one 12½" end of an H; press seams toward H.

3. Sew a C strip to opposite short ends and I strips to opposite long sides of the pieced center; press seams toward C and I strips.

4. Repeat steps 1–3 to complete four place mat tops.

5. Layer, quilt and bind each place mat referring to Finishing Your Quilt on page 96. Δ

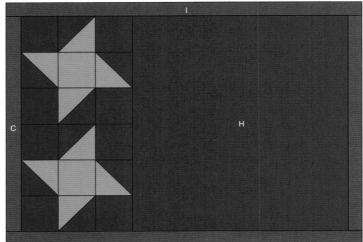

Star Bright Place Mat
Placement Diagram 19" x 13½"

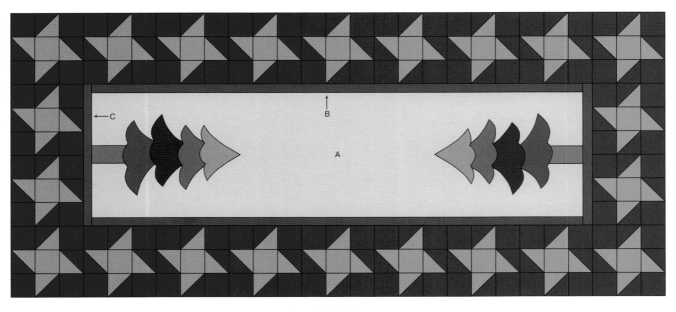

Star Bright Runner
Placement Diagram 54" x 24"

Trunk
Cut 2 brown check scrap

Tree Motif
Cut 2 each piece green print scraps

Give & Take Ornaments

DESIGN BY DAPHNE GREIG

Careful cutting results in positive and negative shapes in this quilt and bag using the give-and-take appliqué method.

Positive Ornament
7" x 9" Block
Make 4 for quilt
Make 1 for bag

Negative Ornament
7" x 9" Block
Make 5 for quilt

Project Specifications

Skill Level: Beginner
Quilt Size: 35" x 41"
Bag Size: 13½" x 16"
Block Size: 7" x 9"
Number of Blocks: 9 for quilt;
    1 for bag

Materials

- 1/3 yard red star print
- 3/8 yard red floral print
- 5/8 yard black/red print
- 1/8 yard cream/gold metallic
- 11/8 yard coordinating stripe
- Backing 41" x 47"
- Backing 41" x 47"
- All-purpose thread to match fabric
- Red embroidery thread
- Quilting or clear nylon thread
- 2 yards gold braided cord
- 1½ yards 12"-wide fusible web
- 1¼ yards fabric stabilizer
- Basic sewing tools and supplies

Cutting

1. Cut one 2" by fabric width strip from red star print. Subcut strip into 16 (2") G squares.

2. Cut one 4½" by fabric width strip from red star print. Subcut strip into four 4½" I squares.

3. Cut one 9½" by fabric width strip from red floral print. Subcut strip into five 7½" x 9½" B rectangles.

4. Cut six 1¼" by fabric width black/red print D/E strips.

5. Cut four 2¼" by fabric width black/red print strips for binding.

6. Cut two 9½" by fabric width cream/gold metallic strips. Subcut strips into 10 (7½" x 9½") A rectangles.

7. Cut six 1¼" by fabric width cream/gold C/F strips.

8. Cutting along length of coordinating stripe, cut two each 4½" x 33½" H, 4½" x 27½" J, 4" x 9½" K borders; one each 3½" x 14½" L and 5½" x 14½" M borders and one 14½" x 17½" bag backing N.

Completing the Blocks

1. Cut five 7½" x 9½" rectangles fusible web.

2. Center and trace one ornament design onto each rectangle, aligning top of pattern with top edge of rectangles; do not cut out.

3. Fuse the traced rectangles to the wrong side of the B rectangles, matching outer edges; let cool.

4. Starting at the top edge as shown in Figure 1 and using a sharp pair of scissors, cut continuously on the traced line to make two shapes—one positive ornament shape and one negative B rectangle shape as shown in Figure 2.

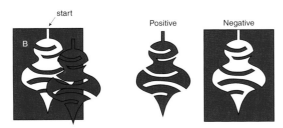

Figure 1   **Figure 2**

5. Fold and lightly crease five A rectangles to mark the vertical centers.

6. Arrange and fuse one positive ornament shape on each creased A rectangle, matching the top and bottom centers of the ornament to the creased line, as shown in Figure 3, to create five Positive Ornament blocks.

Figure 3

7. Arrange and fuse the negative B rectangle shapes onto the remaining A rectangles to create five Negative Ornament blocks.

8. Cut 10 (7" x 9") rectangles fabric stabilizer; pin one to the back of each block.

9. Using red embroidery thread, set your machine to a narrow zigzag stitch and sew the edge of the positive and negative shapes as shown in Figure 4 to complete the blocks; remove fabric stabilizer.

Figure 4

Completing the Bag

1. Sew a K strip to opposite sides of a Positive Ornament block; press seams toward K strips.

2. Sew L to the bottom and M to the top of the bordered block; press seams toward L and M strips.

3. Place the N backing piece right sides together with the pieced top. Referring to Figure 5, mark a line 1" down from the top edge and another line 1" from the marked line; repeat on opposite edge. Using a ½" seam allowance, stitch from the top edge of M to the first marked line; secure stitching. Begin stitching again at the second marked line and stitch all around bag to the next marked line; secure stitching. Begin stitching after the next marked line to leave two 1" openings in the M side seams of the bag. Turn right side out.

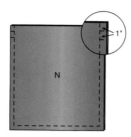

Figure 5

4. Fold the top raw edge of the bag ¼" to the inside and press. Turn ¾" to the inside; press and stitch to make the top casing.

5. Cut the cord into two 36" pieces; attach a safety pin to one end of one piece. Insert into one side opening and feed through the casing all around the top of the bag, returning to the beginning side; remove the safety pin and knot the two ends together.

6. Repeat step 5 with the second piece of cord in the opposite side opening. Pull ends of cord to close the top of the bag.

Completing the Quilt

1. Sew a C/F strip to a D/E strip with right sides together along length; press seams toward darker strip. Repeat to make six strip sets.

2. Subcut strip sets into 12 (7½") C-D units and 12 (9½") E-F units as shown in Figure 6.

Figure 6

3. Join one Positive Ornament block with two Negative Ornament blocks and four E-F units to make an X row as shown in Figure 7; press seams toward E-F units. Repeat to make two X rows.

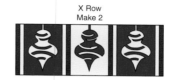

Figure 7

4. Join one Negative Ornament block with two Positive Ornament blocks and four E-F units to make a Y row as shown in Figure 8; press seams toward E-F units.

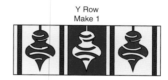

Figure 8

5. Join three C-D units with four G squares to make a sashing row as shown in Figure 9; press seams toward C-D units. Repeat to make four sashing rows.

Figure 9

6. Join the X and Y rows with the sashing rows to complete the pieced center referring to the Placement Diagram; press seams toward the sashing rows.

7. Sew an H strip to opposite long sides of the pieced center; press seams toward H strips.

8. Sew an I square to each end of each J strip; press seams toward J strips.

9. Sew an I-J strip to the top and bottom of the pieced center to complete the pieced top; press seams toward the I-J strips.

10. Layer, quilt and bind referring to Finishing Your Quilt on page 96. Δ

Give & Take Ornaments
Placement Diagram 35" x 41"

Give & Take Ornament Gift Bag
Placement Diagram 13½" x 16"

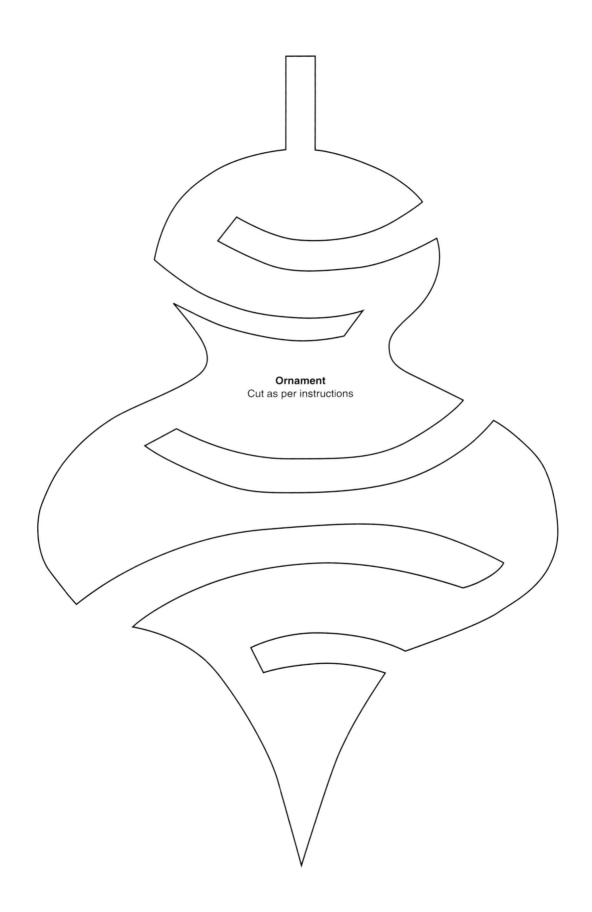

Ornament
Cut as per instructions

Winter Magic

DESIGN BY ANN LAUER FOR GRIZZLY GULCH GALLERY

Brighten up the longest night of the year with a beautiful bargello runner.

Project Specifications

Skill Level: Intermediate
Runner Size: 51½" x 20"

Materials

- 3/8 yard lightest blue
- 3/8 yard light blue
- 3/8 yard medium blue
- 3/8 yard dark blue
- 3/8 yard darkest blue
- 1½ yards white
- 1¾ yards backing fabric
- Batting 56" x 24"
- All-purpose thread to match fabrics
- 1¾ yards flannel with a grid or very thin batting with hand-drawn grid as per instructions
- 24 (4mm) hot-fix crystals
- 24 (3mm) hot-fix crystals
- Spray adhesive or safety pins
- 2 appliqué pressing sheets
- Sewing machine walking foot
- Basic sewing tools and supplies

Project Notes

Figure 1 designates each blue fabric and its initial placement within the strip set. Refer to Figure 1 as you lay out the full-length fabric strips.

Figure 1

You will be adding the strips to the layered gridded flannel, or batting and backing in a quilt-as-you-go method, so that when you finish stitching the top, your quilting will be done.

Use gridded flannel or very thin batting. The grid eliminates the need to draw guidelines on the batting.

Cutting

1. From each of the five blue fabrics, cut two 4½" by fabric width strips; labeling the fabrics 1–5, lightest to darkest, and referring to Figure 1.

2. Enlarge and trace the tree appliqué pattern onto the paper side of the fusible web. **Note:** *You may need to draw the tree in a couple of sections so that it fits on the fusible web.* Cut out pattern, leaving a margin all around.

3. Trace the snowflake shapes onto the paper side of the fusible web, leaving ½" between pieces; cut out shapes, leaving a margin around each one.

4. Iron the snowflake and tree shapes onto the wrong side of white, butting the fusible-web tree-shape pieces end to end to make the shape continuous. Cut on marked lines and set aside.

5. From the backing fabric, cut a 56" x 24" back.

Sewing Strip Sets & Tubes

1. Straighten fabric strips and lay out the five blue fabrics in order from light to dark with the lightest being fabric 1 and the darkest being fabric 5. **Note:** *For reference, cut a ½" swatch of each fabric and staple to a piece of paper and identify by the assigned number.*

2. Sew one strip of each blue fabric Nos. 1–5 together along length in numerical order to make a strip set, keeping ends even at one end, again referring to Figure 1; press seam toward fabric 1. Make a second

identical strip set and press seams away from fabric 1. **Note:** *When pressing, press first from the back, and then from the front.*

3. Sew the long edges of one set together to make a tube; repeat with the second set to make a second tube. Press seams in the same direction as previous, pressing on each tube.

Preparing Backing & Batting

1. Place the backing piece wrong side up on a flat surface; place batting on top.

2. If using gridded flannel, lay flannel on top of backing fabric aligning a grid line even with the top and left edges of the fabric. If using only very thin batting without the gridded flannel, draw a straight line from top to bottom 2" in from the left edge as shown in Figure 2; continue drawing lines every 4" across the batting. Draw a horizontal line across the top 2" in from the edge; continue drawing lines every 4" below it. Layer marked side up on the backing.

Figure 2

3. Secure the layers with basting spray or with safety pins every 10", pinning on the flannel/batting side.

Cutting the Strip Tubes

1. Lay the stitched full-length tubes wrong sides out on a cutting mat, carefully folding on a seam line; label one tube Odd and the other Even. Make straightening cuts along the left edge, removing all selvages. Set aside the tubes to make the final cuts.

2. Referring to Figure 3 for sizes to cut, cut a total of seven segments, cutting odd-numbered cuts from the Odd tube and even-numbered cuts from the Even tube to ensure that the opposing seams will nest together as they are sewn; straighten as needed when cutting. Label each segment with the assigned segment number; arrange segments in numerical order. For example, make your initial cut on the Odd tube at 6". Label it segment 1. Cut segment 2 from the Even tube at 8". Continue cutting and labeling all seven segments.

3. Open each segment between strips as indicated in Figure 3. For example: For segment 1, open the seam between fabrics 4 and 5 referring to Figure 4. Fabric 4 will be at the top of the segment and Fabric 5 will be at the bottom of the segment. Open segment 2 between fabrics 3 and 4. Segment 2 will have fabric 3 at the top and fabric 4 at the bottom. The seams opened are always adjacent to the previously opened seam—shifting either up or down the strip set. Refer to Figure 4 for segments.

Segment cut No.	Tube	Cut width	Separate seam between fabric Nos.
1	Odd	6"	4 & 5
2	Even	8"	3 & 4
3	Odd	9"	2 & 3
4	Even	11"	1 & 2
5	Odd	8"	2 & 3
6	Even	7"	1 & 2
7	Odd	6"	1 & 5

Figure 3

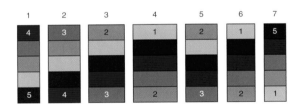

Figure 4

4. Attach a walking foot on your machine.

5. Lay segment 1 on the flannel/batting even with the left vertical line 2" in from the edge and with the top of fabric 4 even with the top horizontal line 2" from the edge as shown in Figure 5. Pin in place and stitch 1/8" from left edge to anchor in place.

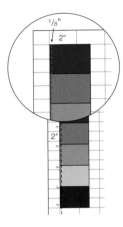

Figure 5

6. Place segment 2 right sides together with segment 1 as shown in Figure 6; match strip seams from segment 1 to segment 2 and align on top and right edges, again referring to Figure 6. Pin at each seam.

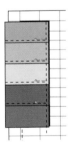

Figure 6

7. Stitch the seam through all layers including flannel/batting and backing; carefully fold segment 2 open as shown in Figure 7 and lightly press it flat.

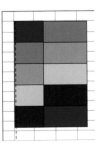

Figure 7

8. Repeat steps 6 and 7 to add all segments.

9. As you lay each new segment on the previous segment, pin carefully and be sure that the top edges align with the top horizontal line. As you open the segments, the cut edge should be parallel to the vertical registration lines. If the segments are beginning to slant or bow, make a slight adjustment (sew a slightly wider or narrower seam) as soon as possible.

10. As you join the segments, compare your design with the Placement Diagram and the project photo to be sure that you are shifting the strips correctly.

11. Stitch 1/8" from the right side edge of the final segment.

12. Use a large square template or right-angle ruler to check that your runner is square; straighten as needed. Trim flannel/batting and backing even with the top.

Finishing the Runner

1. Bind edges referring to Finishing Your Quilt on page 96.

2. Remove backing from the appliqué shapes. Position and fuse the tree and snowflake shapes on the pieced background referring to the Placement Diagram and project photo for positioning.

3. Edge-stitch the large snowflakes using white thread. Drop the feed dogs on your machine and stitch down the center of the small snowflakes, and then stitch on and off each point to give the snowflake a fluffy look.

4. Add hot-fix crystals on snowflake shapes as desired referring to manufacturer's instructions and referring to the pattern for positioning of the small and large crystals. △

Winter Magic
Placement Diagram 51½" x 20"

Small Snowflake
Cut 2 white solid

Stylized Tree
Enlarge 450 percent
Cut 1 white solid
Note: *Pattern is reversed for fusible appliqué.*

Large Snowflake
Cut 3 white solid

Winter Snowflake

DESIGN BY BARBARA CLAYTON

Here's a quilt of apparent intricacies—but the end result is worth the extra time and effort.

Project Specifications

Skill Level: Advanced
Wall Quilt Size: Approximately 44½" x 44½"
Block Size: 15½" x 15½"
Number of Blocks: 4

Materials

- ½ yard white solid
- 1 yard light blue print (#1)
- ¾ yard medium blue print (#2)
- ½ yard dark teal print (#3)
- ½ yard medium blue/navy floral print (#4)
- ½ yard navy print (#5)
- Backing 50" x 50"
- Thin batting 50" x 50"
- Rotary-cutting tools
- All-purpose threads to blend with fabrics
- Clear nylon monofilament
- White and medium blue quilting thread
- Stylus
- Basic sewing tools and supplies

Winter Snowflake
15½" x 15½" Block
Make 4

Project Note

Before cutting, label fabrics with numbers 1–5 referring to materials list. Blue fabrics are referred to by number in cutting and assembly instructions. Label pieces and group pieces cut from each fabric together.

Cutting

1. Prepare templates using patterns given.

2. From white solid, cut eight 1½" by fabric width strips, two strips each 2" x 30½" and 2" x 33½" for border.

3. Cut 32 each C and D from white solid.

4. From fabric 1, cut four 1½" by fabric width strips and two strips each 3½" x 33½" and 3½" x 39½" for border.

5. Cut eight A and 32 E from fabric 1.

6. Cut eight 47/8" corner squares and two 7½" squares from fabric 1. Cut the 7½" squares in half on both diagonals to make eight middle triangles.

7. From fabric 2, cut four 1½" by fabric width strips, eight A, 32 E and 28 F pieces.

8. Cut eight 47/8" corner squares and two 7½" squares from fabric 2. Cut each 7½" square in half on both diagonals to make eight middle triangles.

9. From fabric 3, cut 16 B and 28 F pieces.

10. From fabric 4, cut 16 B and 28 F pieces.

11. From fabric 5, cut 16 A and 28 F pieces.

Completing the Blocks

1. For light blue print background block, piece star center by joining A pieces, alternating fabric 1 and 5 colors as shown in Figure 1. Sew from dots to the center points. Press seams open.

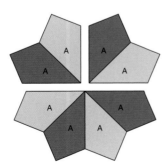

Figure 1

2. Add fabric 4 B star pieces to star centers as shown in Figure 2. Start and end stitching at dots; press.

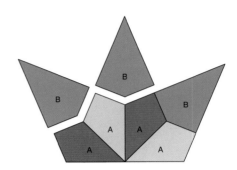

Figure 2

3. Sew one each 1½" white and fabric 1 strips right sides together on one long side. Press toward fabric 1. Repeat with two more strips.

4. Rotary-cut 16 G rectangles by aligning the diagonal line on the G template with the seam line on one pair of strips. Reverse the template and cut 16 reversed G (GR) from the second pair of strips.

5. Sew one pair of G units and one pair of GR units as shown in Figure 3.

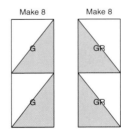

Make 8   Make 8

Figure 3

6. Add E triangles, C square and D diamonds as shown in Figure 4.

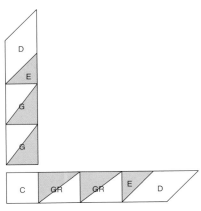

Figure 4

7. Sew strips to corner square as shown in Figure 5. Repeat for four corners.

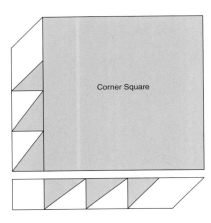

Figure 5

8. Set corners into star as shown in Figure 6.

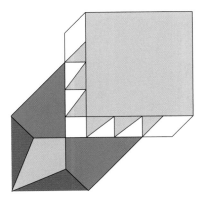

Figure 6

9. Sew one pair of G units and one pair of G units reversed, again referring to Figure 3. Add E triangles and C square as shown in Figure 7. Repeat for four strips each.

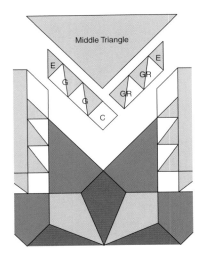

Figure 7

10. Join pieces, again referring to Figure 7. Set the longer strip into the star unit first and then the shorter. Then set in the middle triangle; press. The middle triangles tend to shrink toward the center. For that reason they were cut slightly larger than necessary. When construction is complete, trim block to 15½" square.

11. Repeat steps 1–10 for second block.

12. For medium blue print background blocks, repeat steps 1–10 using fabric 2 A, E, corner squares, middle triangles and 1½" strips; fabric 3 B and fabric 5 A to make two blocks.

13. Referring to Placement Diagram for color placement, join four blocks to make two rows; join rows to complete the pieced center. Press row seams in opposite directions and the pieced center seam in one direction.

Completing the Borders

1. Sew 2" x 30½" white strips to top and bottom, and 2" x 33½" white strips to sides of the pieced center; press seams away from white border strips.

2. Sew fabric 1 3½" x 33½" and 3½" x 39½" strips to quilt as in step 1; press seam allowance away from white border strips.

Figure 8

3. For Dresden Plate borders, sew a strip sequence of 23 F pieces, alternating fabrics 2–5, as shown in Figure 8. Repeat for four strips.

4. For border corners, sew two fabric 2 F pieces and one F each of fabrics 3–5 together for border corner sections as shown in Figure 9. Repeat to make four corner sections.

Figure 9

5. Join the four sides of Dresden Plate borders by sewing corner sections between adjacent sides. This will make a large, square border frame. Carefully mark the centers of all sides of border and quilt. Match centers and pin border in place.

6. Turn the inside edges of the border under ¼" all the way around the quilt, carefully folding the points to make them sharp. Place on the light blue border and machine-stitch in place as an appliqué with clear nylon monofilament and a narrow blind-hemstitch. Trim excess light blue border fabric away from under Dresden Plate border to ¼".

Completing the Quilt

1. Mark quilting lines ¼" from outer edges of corner squares and middle triangles. Referring to Placement Diagram, mark diagonal lines ¾" apart on corner squares of each block. Mark lines ¾" apart, perpendicular to border on middle triangles. Transfer the Diamond Quilting Pattern to the white border.

2. Place quilt top and backing right sides together. Pin corners and several places in the center. Place pinned layers on batting square and pin in many places to secure. Sew around perimeter ¼" from edges of Dresden Plate border, leaving an area open on one side for turning.

3. Trim excess batting and backing; trim points and clip curves. Turn right side out and carefully poke out each point using the stylus; press with a warm iron. Turn edges of opening under ¼" and close with hand stitches. Baste layers for quilting.

4. If machine quilting, use a walking foot and clear nylon monofilament. Quilt in the ditch along all seam lines.

5. If hand quilting, stitch in the ditch with white thread. With medium blue thread, hand-quilt diamond pattern on white border, ¼" from edge of white border and inner edges of Dresden Plate border. Quilt ¼" from seam lines of center stars, and corner squares and middle triangles of blocks with white thread on fabric 2 background blocks and with medium blue thread on fabric 1 background blocks. △

Winter Snowflake
Placement Diagram Approximately 44¹/₂" x 44¹/₂"

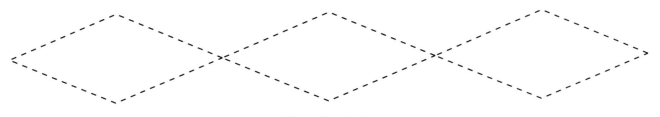

Winter Snowflake
Diamond Quilting Pattern

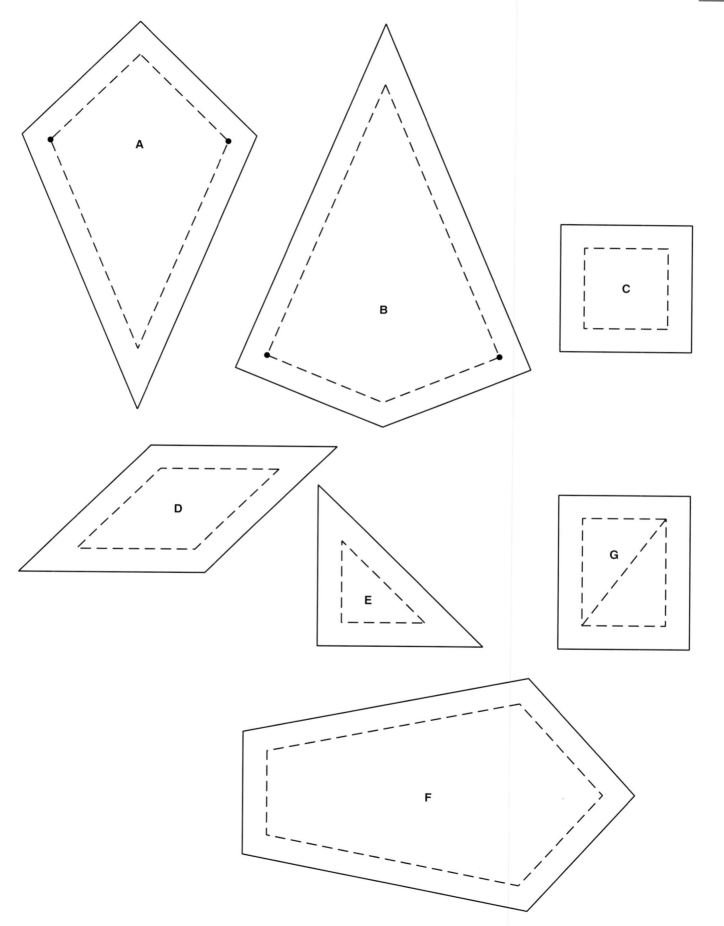

Ornament Wall Hanging

DESIGN BY CAROLYN S. VAGTS

Make this small embellished wall quilt to hang in your office cubicle or in a small space in your home.

Project Specifications

Skill Level: Intermediate
Wall Hanging: 17" x 19"

Materials

- Scraps brown, green, red and gold batiks
- 1 fat quarter gold metallic solid
- 1 fat quarter cream tonal
- 3/8 yard green scroll print
- Backing 23" x 25"
- Batting 23" x 25"
- All-purpose thread to match fabrics
- Quilting thread
- Gold metallic thread
- ½ yard 18"-wide fusible web
- Gold bugle beads and red seed beads or other embellishments
- Basic sewing tools and supplies

Cutting

1. Trace the appliqué shapes given onto the paper side of the fusible web as directed on patterns; cut out shapes, leaving a margin around each one.

2. Fuse shapes to the wrong side of fabrics as directed on each piece for color; cut out shapes on traced lines. Set aside.

3. From gold metallic, cut two 1¼" x 15½" B borders and two 1¼" x 13½" C borders.

4. Cut one 13½" x 15½" A rectangle from cream tonal.

5. Cut two 2½" by fabric width strips from green scroll print. Subcut strips into two 15½" D strips and two 17½" E strips.

6. Cut two 2¼" by fabric width strips for binding from green scroll print.

Completing the Background

1. Fold each B and C piece in half along length with wrong sides together to make double-layered strips; press.

2. Place the B strips along the long sides of A and machine-baste in place 1/8" from edges. Repeat with the C strips on the top and bottom, folding the ends at an angle to make a mitered corner look as shown in Figure 1.

Figure 1

3. Sew D strips to opposite long sides and E strips to the top and bottom of the A-B-C piece to complete the background; press seams toward D and E strips.

Completing the Appliqué

1. Remove paper backing from appliqué shapes.

2. Arrange needles and branches on A referring to the Placement Diagram for positioning, placing ends of branches under the edge of left-hand B strip. When satisfied with placement, fuse shapes in place.

3. Reduce stitch length to 15 stitches per inch or 1.5; select the needle-down position if you have that option on your machine. Machine straight-stitch close to edges of each fused shape using thread to match fabrics.

4. Cut four 5" pieces gold metallic thread; wind one piece around another to make a double-looping thread. Tie the end into a knot; repeat to make two hanging loops.

5. Hand-stitch the knotted end to the top edges of the branches as if they are holding the ornaments.

6. Straighten out the thread loops and pin a cap shape to the end of the hanging loop; fuse top edge of cap in place, catching the end of the loop.

7. Insert ornament shapes under the bottom of the caps and fuse shapes in place. Machine straight-stitch pieces in place using thread to match fabrics as in step 3.

Completing the Quilt

1. Add some detail stitching to the ornaments using your favorite built-in machine-embroidery stitches referring to lines on ornament shapes as guides for placement of stitching lines and using thread to contrast with ornament (gold on red ornament, red on gold ornament).

2. Add beads to ornaments as desired. ***Note:*** *The sample shown uses gold bugle beads in a cross and X pattern between the lines of embroidery stitches on the gold ornament, using red seed beads at the X tips and in the center as shown in the close-up photo and in Figure 2. Stitch beads in place using thread to match ornaments. The red ornament uses eight gold bugle beads in a spoke pattern with a red seed bead in the center, between the lines of embroidery stitches.*

Figure 2

3. Add detail-stitching lines on ornament caps using gold metallic thread.

4. Layer, quilt and bind referring to Finishing Your Quilt on page 96.

5. A hanging sleeve may be added to the top back side of the quilt, if desired. △

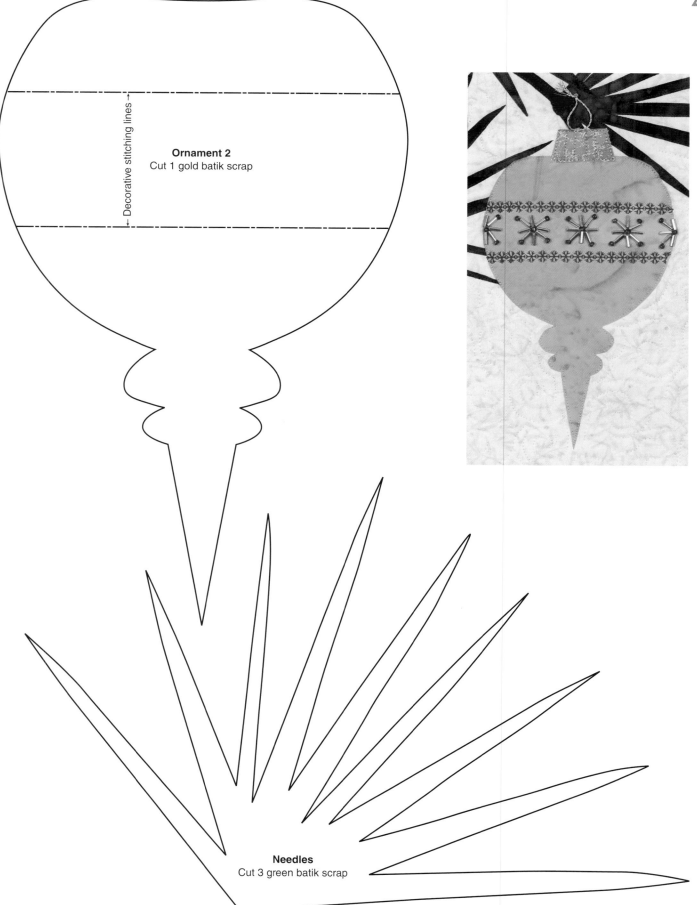

Decorative stitching lines

Ornament 2
Cut 1 gold batik scrap

Needles
Cut 3 green batik scrap

Branches
Cut 1 each brown
batik scrap

Ornament Cap
Cut 2 gold metallic solid

Decorative stitching lines

Ornament 1
Cut 1 red batik scrap

Ornament Wall Hanging
Placement Diagram 17" x 19"

Christmas Hospitality Runner

DESIGN BY JULIA DUNN

Greeting your guests with a seasonal bed runner is a great way to spread holiday cheer.

Red Pineapple
7" x 7" Block
Make 9

Green Pineapple
7" x 7" Block
Make 9

Project Specifications

Skill Level: Beginner
Runner Size: 71" x 22"
Block Size: 7" x 7"
Number of Blocks: 18

Materials

- ½ yard cream plaid
- ¾ yard total cream scraps
- ¾ yard total green scraps
- ¾ yard total red scraps
- 1 yard red print
- Backing 79" x30"
- Batting 79" x 30"
- Neutral-color all-purpose thread
- Quilting thread
- Basic sewing tools and supplies

Cutting

1. Cut four 2¼" by fabric width A strips from cream plaid.

2. Cut one 2¼" by fabric width strips; subcut into two 18" B strips.

3. From cream scraps, cut 72 (1¼" x 3") pieces for areas 6–9 of pineapple paper-piecing pattern. Cut 72 (1¼" x 3½") pieces for areas 14–17 and 72 (1¼" x 4¼") pieces for areas 22–25.

4. From green scraps, cut 36 (1¼" x 2½") pieces for areas 3 and 5 of pineapple paper-piecing pattern. Cut 36 (1¼" x 3") pieces for areas 11 and 13, and 36 (1¼" x 3½") pieces for areas 19 and 21.

5. Cut 18 (3½") squares from green scraps. Cut each square in half on one diagonal to make 36 triangles for areas 27 and 29.

6. Cut nine 2½" squares for area 1 from green scraps.

7. From red scraps, cut 36 (1¼" x 2½") pieces for areas 2 and 4 of pineapple paper-piecing pattern. Cut 36 (1¼" x 3") pieces for areas 10 and 12, and 36 (1¼" x 3½") pieces for areas 18 and 20.

8. Cut 18 (3½") squares from red scraps. Cut each square in half on one diagonal to make 36 triangles for areas 26 and 28.

9. Cut nine 2½" squares from red scraps for area 1.

10. From red print, cut four 2¾" by fabric width C strips, two 2¾" x 22½" D strips and five 2¼" by fabric width strips for binding.

Completing the Blocks

1. Make copies of the paper-piecing pattern given.

2. Set machine stitch length to a short stitch.

3. Position a green 2½" square in the center of the unmarked side of one paper pattern as shown in Figure 1; place a No. 2 red strip right sides together on top of the square.

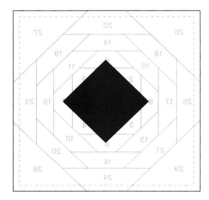

Figure 1

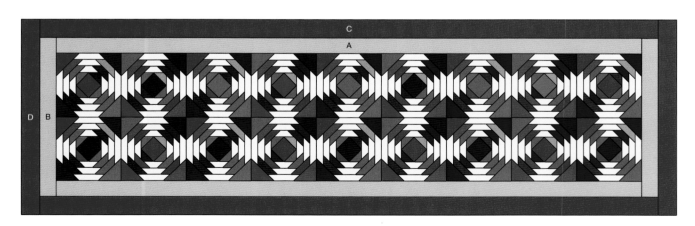

Christmas Hospitality Runner
Placement Diagram 71" x 22"

4. Flip paper over and stitch along the marked line between pieces 1 and 2, making one stitch into areas 6 and 9 on each end of the line as shown in Figure 2.

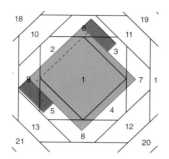

Figure 2

5. Turn the paper over to the fabric side and flip the top strip to the right side; press. Trim strip as shown in Figure 3, leaving ¼" extending into areas 6, 9 and 10.

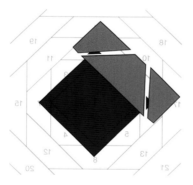

Figure 3

6. Continue sewing, pressing and trimming strips Nos. 3–25. Add Nos. 26–29 triangles to corners to complete one Green Pineapple block.

7. Repeat steps 3–6 to complete a total of nine each Red Pineapple and Green Pineapple blocks.

Completing the Runner

1. Select and join five Green Pineapple blocks with four Red Pineapple blocks to make a row, beginning and ending with a green block; press seams toward the Green Pineapple blocks.

2. Select and join five Red Pineapple blocks with four Green Pineapple blocks to make a row, beginning and ending with a red block; press seams toward the Green Pineapple blocks.

3. Join the two pieced block rows to complete the pieced center; press seam in one direction.

4. Join the A strips on short ends with a diagonal seam as shown in Figure 4 to make one long strip; trim seam to ¼" and press seam open.

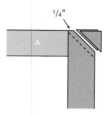

Figure 4

5. Subcut the A strip into two 63½" A strips.

6. Sew an A strip to opposite long sides and B strips to the short ends of the pieced center; press seams toward A and B strips.

7. Repeat step 4 with C strips and subcut strip into two 67" C strips.

8. Sew a C strip to opposite long sides and D strips to the short ends of the pieced center; press seams toward C and D strips to complete the pieced top.

9. Layer, quilt and bind referring to Finishing Your Quilt on page 96. △

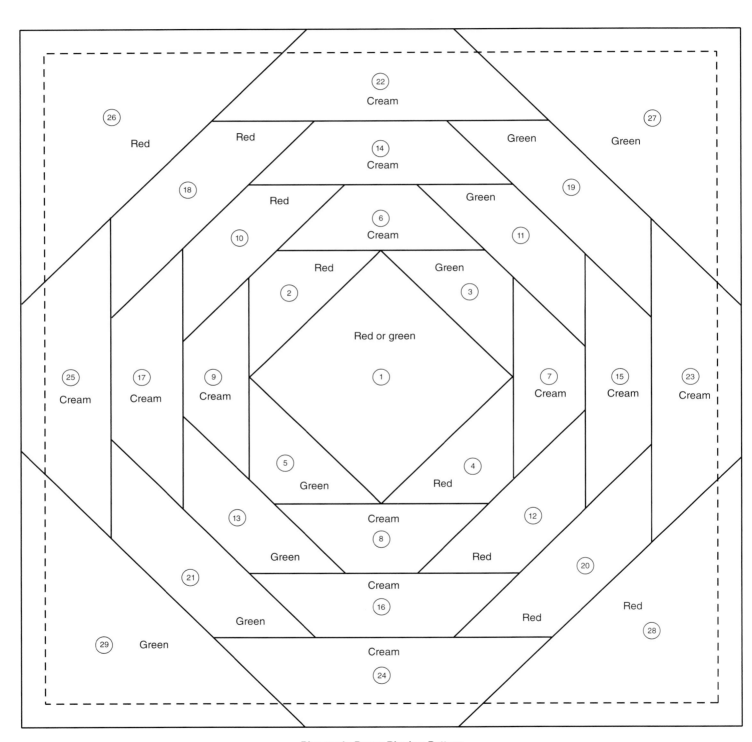

Pineapple Paper-Piecing Pattern
Make 18 copies

Christmas Counterchange

DESIGN BY CONNIE KAUFFMAN

Select a variety of scraps in Christmas colors
and cream to make this very simple Four-Patch design.

Project Specifications

Skill Level: Beginner
Quilt Size: 59" x 69"
Block Size: 5" x 5"
Number of Blocks: 99

Materials

- 7" x 15" scraps 25 different red/
  burgundy, green and cream fabrics
- ¼ yard green tonal
- 3/8 yard cream print
- 1½ yards burgundy print
- Backing 65" x 75"
- Batting 65" x 75"
- Neutral-color all-purpose thread
- Quilting thread
- Basic sewing tools and supplies

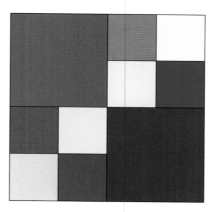

Dark Four-Patch
5" x 5" Block
Make 50

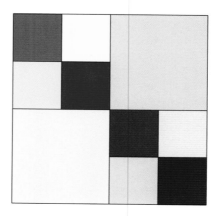

Light Four-Patch
5" x 5" Block
Make 49

Cutting

1. From each red/burgundy and green scrap, cut two 3" A squares and one 1¾" x 14" B strip.

2. From each cream scrap, cut four 3" C squares and two 1¾" x 14" D strips.

3. Cut five 1¾" by fabric width F/G strips cream print.

4. Cut six 1¼" by fabric width H/I strips green tonal.

5. Cut six 5½" by fabric width J strips burgundy print.

6. Cut seven 2¼" by fabric width strips burgundy print for binding.

Piecing Blocks

1. Sew a D strip to a B strip to make a strip set; press seams toward B. Subcut strip set into eight 1¾" B-D segments as shown in Figure 1. Repeat with all B and D strips.

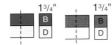

Figure 1

2. To make the Dark Four-Patch blocks, sew a green/cream B-D segment to a red/cream B-D segment as shown in Figure 2; repeat for 100 units.

Figure 2

3. Sew a red/burgundy A to a B-D unit as shown in Figure 3; repeat for 50 units. Repeat with a green A and a B-D unit, again referring to Figure 3 to make 50 units. Press seams toward A.

Make 50 each

Figure 3

4. Join one unit of each color combination to complete one Dark Four-Patch block referring to Figure 4; repeat for 50 blocks. Press seams in one direction.

Figure 4

5. To make the Light Four-Patch blocks, join two red/cream B-D segments as shown in Figure 5; repeat for 49 units. Join two green/cream B-D segments, again referring to Figure 5; repeat for 49 units.

Make 49 each

Figure 5

6. Sew a C square to each B-D unit as shown in Figure 6; press seams toward C.

Figure 6

7. Join the units to complete one Light Four-Patch block as shown in Figure 7; repeat for 49 blocks.

Figure 7

Completing the Top

1. Join four Light Four-Patch blocks and five Dark Four-Patch blocks to make a row referring to Figure 8; press seams toward Dark Four-Patch blocks. Repeat for six rows.

2. Join four Dark Four-Patch blocks and five Light Four-Patch blocks to make a row, again referring to Figure 8; press seams toward Dark Four-Patch blocks. Repeat for five rows.

Make 6

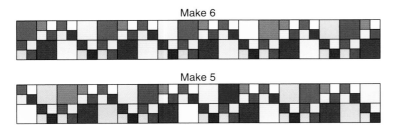

Make 5

Figure 8

3. Join the rows referring to the Placement Diagram to complete the pieced top; press seams in one direction.

4. Join F/G strips on short ends to make one long strip; press seams to one side. Subcut strip into two 55½" F strips and two 48" G strips.

5. Sew an F strip to opposite sides and a G strip to the top and bottom of the pieced center; press seams toward strips.

6. Join H/I strips on short ends to make one long strip; press seams to one side. Subcut strip into two 58" H strips and two 49½" I strips.

7. Sew an H strip to opposite sides and an I strip to the top and bottom of the pieced center; press seams toward H and I strips.

8. Join J strips on short ends to make one long strip; press seams to one side. Subcut strip into four 59½" J strips.

9. Sew a J strip to opposite sides and to the top and bottom of the pieced center; press seams toward J strips.

10. Layer, quilt and bind referring to Finishing Your Quilt on page 96. Δ

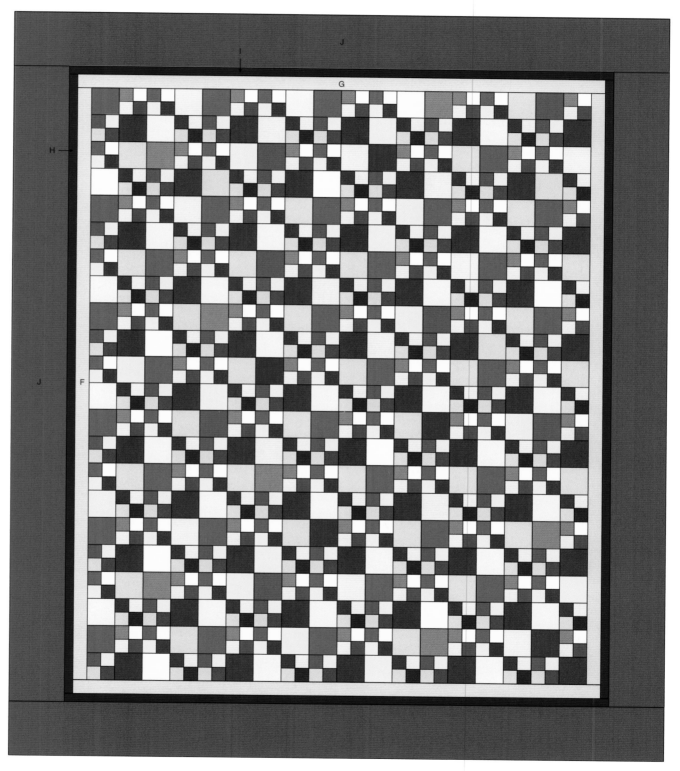

Christmas Counterchange
Placement Diagram 59" x 69"

Holly Jolly Snowmen

DESIGN BY JULIE WEAVER

Pieced trees and appliquéd snowmen make the perfect holiday wall quilt.

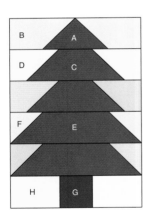

Tree
8" x 12" Block
Make 4

Snowman
8" x 12" Block
Make 5

Project Specifications

Skill Level: Beginner
Quilt Size: 40" x 52"
Block Size: 8" x 12"
Number of Blocks: 9

Materials

- Scraps red, gold, blue, orange, brown and white
- 1/8 yard brown print
- 5/8 yard green print
- 11/8 yards red print
- 13/8 yards total assorted cream/tan tonals
- Backing 46" x 58"
- Batting 46" x 58"
- Black and all-purpose thread to match fabrics
- Quilting thread
- Black embroidery floss
- ¾ yard fusible web
- 13 small star buttons (optional)
- 44 white snowflake buttons (optional)
- Black fine-point permanent fabric pen
- Basic sewing tools and supplies

Cutting

1. Cut the following 2½"-wide pieces from assorted cream/tan tonals: eight 4½" B rectangles, 16 (3½") D rectangles, 16 (2½") F squares and eight 3½" H rectangles.

2. Cut the following 1½"-wide pieces from assorted cream/tan tonals: 10 (4½") J, 20 (8½") K, 16 (6½") L and 10 (10½") M.

3. Cut five 4½" x 6½" I rectangles assorted cream/tan tonals.

4. Cut the following 1½"-wide pieces from assorted cream/tan tonals: 12 each 8½" O and 12½" N strips, and 16 (1½") P squares.

5. Cut four 2½" by fabric width strips green print; subcut strips into four 4½" A and eight each 6½" C and 8½" E rectangles.

6. Cut four 1½" by fabric width strips green print; subcut strips into two 40½" Q strips and two 30½" R strips.

7. Cut four 2½" G squares brown print.

8. Cut four 5½" by fabric width strips red print; subcut strips into two 42½" S strips and two 40½" T strips.

9. Cut five 2¼" by fabric width strips red print for binding.

10. Trace appliqué shapes onto the paper side of the fusible web referring to pattern for number to cut; cut out shapes, leaving a margin around each one. **_Note:_** _The shapes are given in reverse for fusible appliqué. The Corner Snowman Motif will make the two left-facing snowmen. Reverse the patterns to trace the shapes for the two right-facing snowmen._

11. Fuse shapes to the wrong side of assorted scraps as directed on patterns for color and number to cut; cut out shapes on traced lines. Remove paper backing.

12. Draw eyes and X marks on snowmen faces using black fine-point permanent fabric pen.

Completing the Tree Blocks

1. Place a B rectangle right sides together on one end of A as shown in Figure 1; mark a line from the top corner of B to where it intersects with A, again referring to Figure 1.

Figure 1

2. Stitch on the marked line; trim excess seam to ¼" and press B to the right side referring to Figure 2.

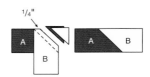

Figure 2

3. Repeat with a second B on the opposite end of A to complete an A-B unit as shown in Figure 3; repeat to make four A-B units.

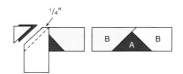

Figure 3

4. Repeat steps 1–3 to make eight each C-D and E-F units as shown in Figure 4.

Figure 4

5. Sew G between two H rectangles to make a G-H unit; press seams toward G. Repeat to make four G-H units.

6. To complete one Tree block, arrange the pieced units as shown in Figure 5. Join the pieced units and press seams in one direction to complete one block; repeat to make four Tree blocks.

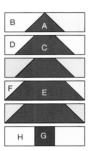

Figure 5

Completing the Snowman Blocks

1. Sew J to opposite short sides of I; press seams toward J.

2. Sew K strips to opposite long sides of the J-I unit; press seams toward K.

3. Continue adding pieces to the short sides, and then long sides, to complete the block background referring to Figure 6, pressing seams toward the most recently added strips after each addition. Repeat to make five block backgrounds.

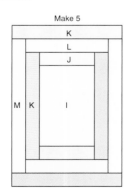

Make 5

Figure 6

4. Center and arrange a snowman motif on each block background with pieces in numerical order and overlapping as necessary. When satisfied with placement, fuse shapes in place.

5. Using black thread, buttonhole-stitch around each fused shape.

6. If desired, sew three small star buttons to the front of each Corner Snowman and one star button to scarf of Center Snowman as shown on patterns.

Completing the Quilt

1. Join one Tree block, two Corner Snowman blocks and four N strips to make a row as shown in Figure 7; press seams toward N strips. Repeat to make two rows.

Make 2

Figure 7

2. Join one Center Snowman block, two Tree blocks and four N strips to make the center row referring to Figure 8; press seams toward N strips.

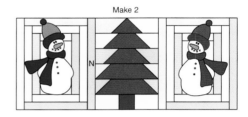

Figure 8

3. Join three O strips with four P squares to make a sashing row as shown in Figure 9; press seams toward O strips. Repeat to make four sashing rows.

Figure 9

4. Join the block rows with the sashing rows referring to the Placement Diagram for positioning; press seams toward sashing strips.

5. Sew Q strips to opposite long sides and R strips to the top and bottom of the pieced center; press seams toward Q and R strips.

6. Sew S strips to opposite long sides and T strips to the top and bottom of the pieced center; press seams toward S and T strips to complete the pieced top.

7. Layer, quilt and bind referring to Finishing Your Quilt on page 96.

8. Hand-stitch snowflake buttons on tree shapes, if desired. △

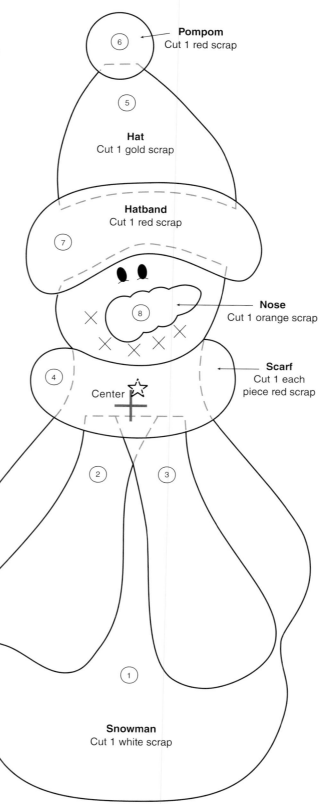

Pompom
Cut 1 red scrap

Hat
Cut 1 gold scrap

Hatband
Cut 1 red scrap

Nose
Cut 1 orange scrap

Scarf
Cut 1 each
piece red scrap

Center

Snowman
Cut 1 white scrap

Center Snowman Motif

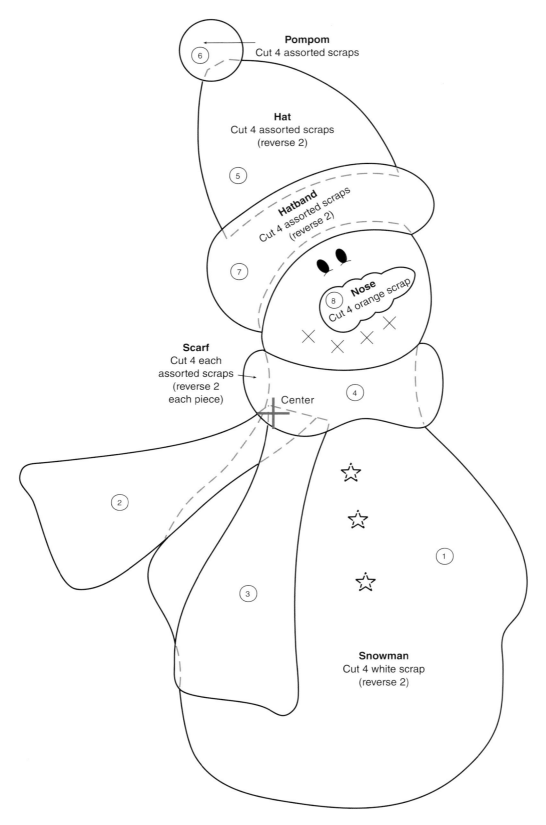

Pompom
Cut 4 assorted scraps

Hat
Cut 4 assorted scraps
(reverse 2)

Hatband
Cut 4 assorted scraps
(reverse 2)

Nose
Cut 4 orange scrap

Scarf
Cut 4 each
assorted scraps
(reverse 2
each piece)

Center

Snowman
Cut 4 white scrap
(reverse 2)

Corner Snowman Motif

Holly Jolly Snowmen
Placement Diagram 40" x 52"

Scrappy Red Christmas

DESIGN BY RUTH SWASEY

A variety of red fabrics combine with white solid to make a striking Christmas quilt.

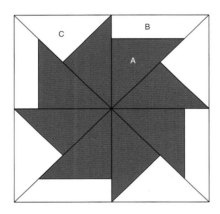

Pinwheel
12" x 12" Block
Make 30

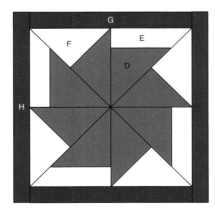

Framed Pinwheel
12" x 12" Block
Make 20

Project Specifications

Skill Level: Intermediate
Quilt Size: 93½" x 110½"
Block Sizes: 12" x 12"
Number of Blocks: 50

Materials

- 20 strips 5" by fabric width red fabrics
- 30 strips 6" by fabric width red fabrics
- 3½ yards red tonal
- 7 yards white solid
- Backing 100" x 117"
- Batting 100" x 117"
- All-purpose thread to match fabrics
- Quilting thread
- Rotary ruler with 45-degree-angle line
- Basic sewing tools and supplies

Cutting

1. Trim the 6" by fabric width strips to 53/8"; subcut each strip into four 53/8" squares. Cut each square in half on one diagonal to make eight A triangles to total 240 A triangles.

2. Trim the 5" by fabric width strips to 45/8"; subcut each strip into four 45/8" squares. Cut each square in half on one diagonal to make eight D triangles to total 160 D triangles.

3. Cut six 67/8" by fabric width strips white solid; subcut strips into 120 (2") B rectangles. Cut one end of each rectangle at a 45-degree angle as shown in Figure 1.

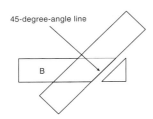

45-degree-angle line

B

Figure 1

4. Cut six 7¼" by fabric width strips white solid; subcut strips into 30 (7¼") squares. Cut each square on both diagonals to make 120 C triangles.

5. Cut four 57/8" by fabric width strips white solid; subcut strips into 80 (1¾") E rectangles. Cut one end of each rectangle at a 45-degree angle, again referring to Figure 1.

6. Cut one 8" by fabric width strip white solid; subcut strip into two 8" squares. Cut each square in half on one diagonal to make four K triangles.

7. Trim the remainder of the 8"-wide strip white solid to 6¼"; subcut strip into four 6¼" squares.

8. Cut three 6¼" by fabric width strips white solid; subcut strips into 16 (6¼") squares. Cut each of these squares and those cut in step 7 on both diagonals to make 80 F triangles.

9. Cut three 153/8" by fabric width strips white solid; subcut strips into five 153/8" squares. Cut each square on both diagonals to make 18 I triangles.

10. Cut 10 (25/8") by fabric width strips white solid. Join strips on short ends to make one long strip; press seams open. Subcut strip into two 102½" L strips and two 89¾" M strips.

11. Cut four 5½" by fabric width strips white solid; subcut strips into 23 (5½") squares. Cut each square on both diagonals to make 92 N triangles.

12. Cut two 10½" by fabric width strips red tonal; subcut strips into 40 (1½") G strips.

13. Cut three 12½" by fabric width strips red tonal; subcut strips into 58 (1½") H strips.

14. Cut one 14½" by fabric width strip red tonal; subcut strip into 22 (1½") J strips.

15. Cut four 5½" by fabric width strips red tonal; subcut strips into 22 (5½") squares and two 51/8" squares. Cut each 5½" square on both diagonals to make 88 O triangles and each 51/8" square in half on one diagonal to make four P triangles.

16. Cut 10 (2¼") by fabric width strips red tonal for binding.

Completing the Pinwheel Blocks

1. To complete one block, sew B to A as shown in Figure 2; press seam toward A. Repeat to make four matching A-B units.

Make 4

B

A

Figure 2

2. Select four A pieces to match those used in the A-B units. Sew C to A as shown in Figure 3; press seam toward A. Repeat to make four A-C units.

Make 4

C A

Figure 3

3. Sew an A-B unit to an A-C unit to complete a block quarter as shown in Figure 4; press seams toward the A-B unit. Repeat to make four quarter units.

Make 4

Figure 4

4. Join two quarter units to make a row referring to Figure 5; press seam toward the A-C unit. Repeat to make two rows.

Make 2

Figure 5

5. Join the rows to complete one Pinwheel block referring to the block drawing; press seam in one direction. Repeat to make 30 blocks.

Completing Framed Pinwheel Blocks

1. Complete 20 pinwheel centers referring to Completing the Pinwheel Blocks and Figure 6 and using D, E and F pieces.

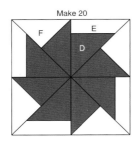

Make 20

F   E

D

Figure 6

2. To complete one Framed Pinwheel block, sew G to two opposite sides and H to the remaining sides of the pieced center referring to the block drawing; press seams toward G and H strips. Repeat to make 20 blocks.

Completing the Quilt

1. Sew an H strip to one side of I as shown in Figure 7; press seams toward H.

J   H

I

Figure 7

2. Sew J to the remaining side of I, aligning one end with the square end of H, again referring to Figure 7; press seams toward J.

3. Trim H and J ends even with I as shown in Figure 8 to complete an H-I-J unit; repeat to make 18 units.

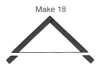

Make 18

Figure 8

4. Center and sew J to the long side of each K triangle to complete four J-K units as shown in Figure 9; press seams toward J.

J   K

Figure 9

5. Trim the J strips even with the edges of K, again referring to Figure 9.

Scrappy Red Christmas
Placement Diagram 93½" x 110½"

6. Arrange and join the pieced blocks in diagonal rows with the H-I-J and J-K triangle units as shown in Figure 10; press seams in adjoining rows in opposite directions.

Figure 10

7. Join the rows to complete the pieced center; press seams in one direction.

8. Sew L strips to opposite long sides and M strips to the top and bottom of the pieced center; press seams toward L and M strips.

9. Join 21 N and 20 O triangles as shown in Figure 11, to complete the top strip; press seams toward N. Repeat to make the bottom strip.

Figure 11

10. Center and sew the N-O strips to the top and bottom of the pieced center referring to the Placement Diagram; press seams toward M strips.

11. Repeat step 9 with 25 N and 24 O triangles to make a side strip; press seams toward N. Repeat to make two side strips.

12. Sew the N-O strips to opposite sides of the pieced center referring to the Placement Diagram; press seams toward L strips.

13. Sew a P triangle to each corner to complete the pieced top; press seams toward P triangles.

14. Layer, quilt and bind referring to Finishing Your Quilt on page 96. △

Redesign Nine

DESIGN BY BEV GETSCHEL

Give this design a try in holiday colors or your favorite scrappy color combination.

Bed Quilt

Project Specifications

Skill Level: Beginner
Quilt Size: 84" x 102"
Block Size: 9" x 9"
Number of Blocks: 80

Materials

- 7/8 yard red tonal
- 1 yard light green fern print
- 3¼ yards total light green prints and tonals
- 4¾ yards red prints and tonals
- Backing 90" x 108"
- Batting 90" x 108"
- Neutral-color all-purpose thread
- Quilting thread
- Basic sewing tools and supplies

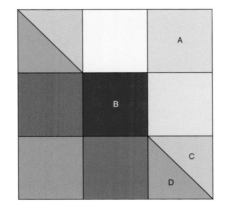

Split Nine-Patch
9" x 9" Block
Make 76

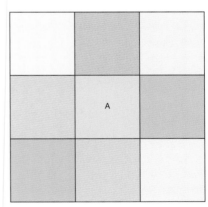

Nine-Patch
9" x 9" Block
Make 4

Cutting

1. From red tonal, cut 10 (2¼" by fabric width) strips for binding.

2. Cut nine 3½" by fabric width F/G strips from light green fern print.

3. From light green prints and tonals, cut 264 (3½") A squares and 76 (37/8") squares. Cut each 37/8" square in half on one diagonal to make 152 C triangles.

4. From red prints and tonals, cut 424 (3½") B squares and 76 (37/8") squares. Cut each 37/8" square in half on one diagonal to make 152 D triangles.

Completing the Nine-Patch Blocks

1. Select nine A squares; join three to make a row. Repeat to make three rows; press seams in one direction.

2. Join the rows with seams in opposite directions to complete one Nine-Patch block; press seams in one direction.

3. Repeat steps 1 and 2 to complete four Nine-Patch blocks.

Completing the Split Nine-Patch Blocks

1. Select three A squares, four B squares and two each C and D triangles.

2. Sew C to D along the diagonal to make a C-D unit as shown in Figure 1; press seam toward D. Repeat to make two C-D units.

Figure 1

3. Arrange and join the C-D units with the A and B squares in rows as shown in Figure 2; press seams of the center row in the opposite direction from the top and bottom rows.

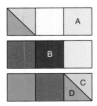

Figure 2

4. Join the rows as arranged to complete one Split Nine-Patch block; press seams in one direction.

5. Repeat steps 1–4 to complete 76 Split Nine-Patch blocks.

Completing the Quilt

1. Join two Split Nine-Patch blocks to make an X block unit as shown in Figure 3; press seam in one direction. Repeat to make 28 X block units.

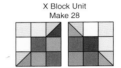

Figure 3

2. Join one Nine-Patch block with one Split Nine-Patch block to make a Y block unit referring to Figure 4; press seam toward Nine-Patch block. Repeat to make two Y block units and two reverse Y block units.

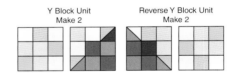

Figure 4

3. Join two Split Nine-Patch blocks to make a Z block unit as shown in Figure 5; press seam in one direction. Repeat to make four Z and four reverse Z block units.

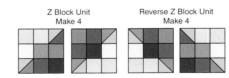

Figure 5

4. Join four X block units to make an X row as shown in Figure 6; press seams in one direction. Repeat to make four X rows.

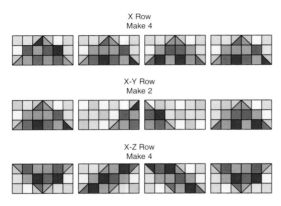

X Row
Make 4

X-Y Row
Make 2

X-Z Row
Make 4

Figure 6

5. Join two X, one Y and one reverse Y block units to make an X-Y row, again referring to Figure 6; press seams in one direction. Repeat to make two X-Y rows.

6. Join two X, one Z and one reverse Z block units to make an X-Z row, again referring to Figure 6; press seams in one direction. Repeat to make four X-Z rows.

7. Arrange and join the rows referring to the Placement Diagram for positioning; press seams in adjoining rows in opposite directions.

8. Join the rows as arranged to complete the pieced center; press seams in one direction.

9. Join the F/G strips on short ends to make one long strip; press seams open. Subcut strip into two 90½" F strips and two 78½" G strips.

10. Sew an F strip to opposite long sides and G strips to the top and bottom of the pieced center; press seams toward F and G strips.

11. Join 32 B squares to make a side strip; repeat to make two strips. Press seams in one direction.

12. Sew a side strip to opposite sides of the pieced center; press seams toward F strips.

13. Join 28 B squares to make the top strip; repeat to make the bottom strip. Press seams in one direction. Sew a strip to the top and bottom of the pieced center; press seams toward G strips to complete the pieced top.

14. Layer, quilt and bind referring to Finishing Your Quilt on page 96.

Bed Runner

Project Specifications

Skill Level: Beginner
Runner Size: 40" x 16"
Block Size: 6" x 6"
Number of Blocks: 12

Materials

1/3 yard light green tonal
½ yard total light green prints and tonals
7/8 yard total red prints and tonals
Backing 46" x 22"
Batting 46" x 22"
Neutral-color and multicolored all-purpose thread
Quilting thread
¼ yard fusible web
Basic sewing tools and supplies

Cutting

1. Cut three 2¼" by fabric width strips from light green tonal for binding.

2. Cut 36 (2½") A squares and 12 (27/8") squares from green prints and tonals. Subcut the 27/8" squares in half on one diagonal to make 24 C triangles.

3. Cut 100 (2½") B squares and 12 (27/8") squares from red prints and tonals. Subcut the 27/8" squares in half on one diagonal to make 24 D triangles.

Completing the Split Nine-Patch Blocks

1. Select three A and four B squares and two each C and D triangles.

2. Sew C to D along the diagonal to make a C-D unit as shown in Figure 1; press seam toward D. Repeat to make two C-D units.

Figure 1

3. Arrange and join the C-D units with the A and B squares in rows as shown in Figure 2; press seams of the center row in the opposite direction from the top and bottom rows.

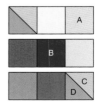

Figure 2

4. Join the rows as arranged to complete one Split Nine-Patch block; press seams in one direction.

5. Repeat Steps 1–4 to complete 12 Split Nine-Patch blocks.

Completing the Top

1. Join two Split Nine-Patch blocks to make an X block unit as shown in Figure 3; press seam in one direction. Repeat to make six X block units.

X Block Unit
Make 6

Figure 3

2. Join two X block units as shown in Figure 4 to complete a Y block unit; press seams in one direction. Repeat to make three Y block units.

Y Block Unit
Make 3

Figure 4

3. Join the Y block units referring to the Placement Diagram to complete the pieced center; press seams in one direction.

Flower
Cut 3 red prints
& tonals

4. Join 18 B squares to make a side strip; repeat to make two strips. Press seams in one direction.

5. Sew a side strip to opposite long sides of the pieced center; press seams toward side strips.

6. Join eight B squares to make an end strip; repeat to make two end strips. Press seams in one direction. Sew end strips to opposite ends of the pieced center; press seams toward end strips.

7. Trace the flower shape onto the paper side of the fusible web as directed on pattern; cut out shapes, leaving a margin around each one.

8. Fuse shapes to the wrong side of red fabrics; cut out shapes on traced lines. Remove paper backing.

9. Fuse a flower shape to center of each Y block unit referring to the Placement Diagram for positioning of shapes.

10. Using multicolored thread, machine zigzag-stitch around each flower shape.

Completing the Runner

1. Sandwich batting between the completed top and prepared backing piece; pin or baste layers together to hold flat.

2. Quilt as desired by hand or machine; remove pins or basting. Trim batting and backing even with the top.

3. Join the binding strips with right sides together on short ends to make one long strip; press seams open.

4. Press the strip in half with wrong sides together along length.

5. Sew the binding to the right side of the runner edges, mitering corners and overlapping ends.

6. Fold binding to the back side and stitch in place to finish.△

Redesign Nine Runner
Placement Diagram 40" x 16"

Redesign Nine
Placement Diagram 84" x 102"

Home for the Holidays

DESIGN BY CHLOE ANDERSON AND COLLEEN REALE FOR TOADUSEW CREATIVE CONCEPTS

Welcome a family member home for the holidays with a new Christmas quilt on his or her bed.

Project Specifications

Skill Level: Beginner
Quilt Size: 60" x 78"

Materials

- ¼ yard dark green print
- ½ yard light green print
- 7/8 yard red print
- 1 yard cream print
- 1 yard coordinating stripe
- 11/8 yards red/green circle print
- 13/8 yards green poinsettia print
- Backing 66" x 84"
- Batting 66" x 84"
- Neutral-color all-purpose thread
- Quilting thread
- Basic sewing tools and supplies

Cutting

1. Cut one 51/8" by fabric width strip from dark green print; subcut strip into four 51/8" squares. Cut each square in half on one diagonal to make eight B triangles.

2. Cut two 67/8" by fabric width strips from light green print; subcut into 12 (67/8") squares. Cut each square in half on one diagonal to make 24 G triangles.

3. Cut one 67/8" by fabric width strip from red print; subcut into four 67/8" squares. Cut each square in half on one diagonal to make eight H triangles.

4. Cut two 6½" by fabric width strips from red print. Subcut strips into four 12½" x 6½" L rectangles and four 6½" M squares.

5. Cut one 51/8" by fabric width strip from red print; subcut strip into four 51/8" squares. Cut each square on one diagonal to make eight A triangles

6. Cut two 67/8" by fabric width strips from cream print. Subcut strips into eight 67/8" squares. Cut each square in half on one diagonal to make 16 F triangles. Subcut remainder of second strip into four 51/8" squares. Cut each square in half on one diagonal to make eight C triangles.

7. Cut two 6½" by fabric width strips from cream print. Subcut into four 6½" K squares and four 12½" x 6½" J rectangles.

8. Cut one 4¾" by fabric width strip from cream print. Subcut strip into four 4¾" D squares.

9. Cut seven 2¼" by fabric width strips from coordinating stripe for binding.

10. Cut three 4½" by fabric width strips from coordinating stripe for P borders.

11. Cut three 5½" by fabric width strips from red/green circle print for Q borders.

12. Cut one 127/8" by fabric width strip from red/green circle print; subcut into two 127/8" squares. Cut each square in half on one diagonal to make four R triangles.

13. Cut one 67/8" by fabric width strip from red/green circle print; subcut into four 67/8" squares. Cut each square in half on one diagonal to make 8 E triangles.

14. Cut six 6½" by fabric width strips from green poinsettia print. Subcut strips into four 6½" x 18½" N rectangles and four 6½" x 24½" O rectangles.

15. Cut one 67/8" by fabric width strip from green poinsettia print; subcut into four 67/8" squares. Cut each square in half on one diagonal to make 8 I triangles.

Completing the Pieced Units

1. Sew A to B along the diagonal to make an A-B unit as shown in Figure 1; press seam toward B. Repeat to make four A-B units.

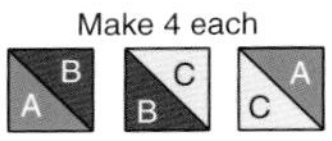

Make 4 each

Figure 1

2. Repeat step 1 to make four B-C units, again referring to Figure 1; press seams toward B.

3. Repeat step 1 to make four A-C units, again referring to Figure 1; press seams toward A.

4. Sew E to F along the diagonal to make an E-F unit as shown in Figure 2; press seam toward E. Repeat to make eight E-F units.

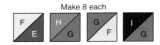

Make 8 each

Figure 2

5. Repeat step 4 to make eight H-G units, again referring to Figure 2; press seams toward H.

6. Repeat step 4 to make eight F-G units, again referring to Figure 2; press seams toward G.

7. Repeat step 4 to make eight G-I units, again referring to Figure 2; press seams toward G.

Completing the Quilt

1. Arrange and join the A-B, B-C and A-C units in rows with D as shown in Figure 3; press seams in adjacent rows in opposite directions.

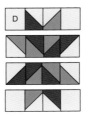

Figure 3

2. Join the rows, again referring to Figure 3; press seams in one direction.

3. Sew R to each side of the pieced unit to complete the center unit as shown in Figure 4; press seams toward R.

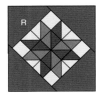

Figure 4

4. Join two E-F units with two K squares to make a K side strip as shown in Figure 5; press seams toward K. Repeat to make two side strips.

Figure 5

5. Sew a K side strip to opposite sides of the pieced center referring to Figure 6; press seams toward K strips.

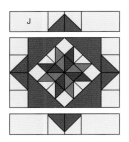

Figure 6

6. Join two E-F units with two J pieces to make a J strip, again referring to Figure 6; press seams toward J pieces. Repeat to make two J strips.

7. Sew the J strips to the top and bottom of the pieced center, again referring to Figure 6; press seams toward J strips.

8. Join two F-G units, two G-H units and two M squares to make an M strip as shown in Figure 7; press seams toward M squares. Repeat to make two M strips.

9. Sew an M strip to opposite sides of the pieced center referring to the Placement Diagram for positioning; press seams toward M strips.

10. Join two F-G units, two G-H units and two L pieces

to make an L strip, again referring to Figure 7. Repeat to make two L strips.

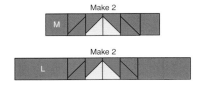

Figure 7

11. Sew an L strip to the top and bottom of the pieced center referring to the Placement Diagram for positioning; press seams toward L strips.

12. Join two G-I units with two N pieces to make an N strip as shown in Figure 8; press seams toward N pieces. Repeat to make two N strips.

13. Sew an N strip to opposite sides of the pieced center referring to the Placement Diagram for positioning; press seams toward N strips.

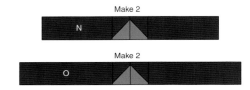

Figure 8

14. Join two G-I units with two O pieces to complete an O strip, again referring to Figure 8; press seams toward O pieces. Repeat to make two O strips.

15. Sew an O strip to the top and bottom of the pieced center referring to the Placement Diagram for positioning; press seams toward O strips.

16. Join the P strips on short ends to make one long strip; press seams open. Subcut strip into two 60½" P strips.

17. Sew a P strip to the top and bottom of the pieced center; press seams toward P strips.

18. Join the Q strips on short ends to make one long strip; press seams open. Subcut strip into two 60½" Q strips.

19. Sew a Q strip to the top and bottom of the pieced center; press seams toward Q strips to complete the pieced top.

20. Layer, quilt and bind referring to Finishing Your Quilt on page 96. △

Home for the Holidays
Placement Diagram 60" x 78"

Quiltmaking Basics

Materials & Supplies

Fabrics

One hundred percent cotton fabrics are recommended for making quilts. Fabrics may be prewashed, depending on your preference, but be sure to do the same thing to all fabrics in the project. Whether you prewash or not, be sure your fabrics are colorfast and won't run onto each other when washed after use.

Fabrics are woven with threads going in a crosswise and lengthwise direction. The threads cross at right angles—the more threads per inch, the stronger the fabric.

The crosswise threads will stretch a little. The lengthwise threads will not stretch at all. Cutting the fabric at a 45-degree angle to the crosswise and lengthwise threads produces a bias edge which stretches a great deal when pulled as shown in Figure 1.

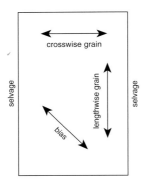

Figure 1

For the patterns in this book that contain templates, pay careful attention careful attention to the grain lines marked with arrows. These arrows indicate that the piece should be placed on the lengthwise grain with the arrow running on one thread as shown in Figure 2.

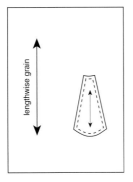

Figure 2

Thread

For most piecing, good-quality cotton or cotton-covered polyester is the thread of choice. Inexpensive polyester threads are not recommended because they can cut the fibers of cotton fabrics.

Choose a color thread that will match or blend with the fabrics in your quilt. For projects pieced with dark- and light-colored fabrics choose a neutral thread color, such as a medium gray, as a compromise between colors. Test by stitching a sample seam.

Batting

Batting is the material used to give a quilt loft or thickness. It also adds warmth.

Some qualities to look for in batting are drapability, resistance to fiber migration, loft and softness.

Tools & Equipment

There are few truly essential tools and little equipment required for quiltmaking. Basics include needles (hand-sewing and quilting betweens), pins (long, thin, sharp pins are best), sharp scissors or shears, a thimble, template materials (plastic or cardboard), marking tools (chalk marker, water-erasable pen and a No. 2 pencil are a few) and a quilting frame or hoop. For piecing and/or quilting by machine, add a sewing machine to the list.

Other sewing basics such as a seam ripper, pincushion, measuring tape and an iron are also necessary. For making strip-pieced quilts, a rotary cutter, mat and speciality rulers are often used.

Construction Methods

Traditional Templates

There are two types of templates—those that include a ¼" seam allowance and those that don't.

Choose the template material and the pattern. Transfer the pattern shapes to the template material with a sharp No. 2 lead pencil. Write the pattern name, piece letter or number, grain line and number to cut for one block or whole quilt on each piece as shown in Figure 3.

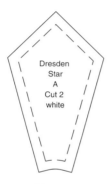

Dresden
Star
A
Cut 2
white

Figure 3

Some patterns require a reversed piece as shown in Figure 4. These patterns are labeled with an R after the piece letter; for example, B and BR. To reverse a template, first cut the fabric with the labeled side up and then with the labeled side down. Or place two layers of fabric with right sides together and cut two pieces at once; one will be reversed.

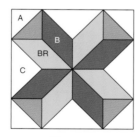

Figure 4

Machine-Piecing

If making templates, include the ¼" seam allowance on the template for machine-piecing. Place template on the wrong side of the fabric and butt pieces together when tracing.

Set machine on 2.5 or 12–15 stitches per inch. Join pieces, beginning and ending sewing at the end of the fabric patch. No backstitching is necessary when machine-stitching.

Quick-Cutting

Templates can be completely eliminated when using a rotary cutter with a plastic ruler and mat to cut fabric strips.

When rotary-cutting strips, straighten raw edges of fabric by folding fabric in half or in fourths across the width as shown in Figure 5. Press down flat; place ruler on fabric square with edge of fabric and make one cut from the folded edge to the outside edge. If strips are not straightened, a wavy strip will result as shown in Figure 6.

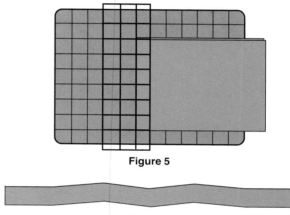

Figure 5

Figure 6

Always cut away from your body, holding the ruler firmly with the non-cutting hand.

Quick-Piecing Method

Lay pieces to be joined under the presser foot of the sewing machine right sides together. Sew an exact ¼" seam allowance to the end of the piece; place another unit right next to the first one and continue sewing, adding a piece after every stitched piece, until all of the pieces are used up as shown in Figure 7.

Figure 7

When sewing is finished, cut the threads that join the pieces apart. Press seam toward the darker fabric.

Finishing Your Quilt

Step 1. Sandwich the batting between the completed top and prepared backing; pin or baste layers together to hold. **Note:** *If using basting spray to hold layers together, refer to instructions on the product container for use.*

Step 2. Quilt as desired by hand or machine; remove pins or basting. Trim excess backing and batting even with quilt top.

Step 3. Join binding strips on short ends to make one long strip. Fold the strip in half along length with wrong sides together; press.

Step 4. Sew binding to quilt edges, mitering corners and overlapping ends. Fold binding to the back side and stitch in place to finish.

Metric Conversion Charts

Metric Conversions

U.S./Canada Measurement		Multiplied by		Metric Measurement
yards	x	.9144	=	metres (m)
yards	x	91.44	=	centimetres (cm)
inches	x	2.54	=	centimetres (cm)
inches	x	25.40	=	millimetres (mm)
inches	x	.0254	=	metres (m)

Canada/U.S. Measurement		Multiplied by		Metric Measurement
centimetres	x	.3937	=	inches
metres	x	1.0936	=	yards

Standard Equivalents

Canada/U.S. Measurement				Metric Measurement
¹⁄₈ inch	=	3.20 mm	=	0.32 cm
¼ inch	=	6.35 mm	=	0.635 cm
³⁄₈ inch	=	9.50 mm	=	0.95 cm
½ inch	=	12.70 mm	=	1.27 cm
⁵⁄₈ inch	=	15.90 mm	=	1.59 cm
¾ inch	=	19.10 mm	=	1.91 cm
⁷⁄₈ inch	=	22.20 mm	=	2.22 cm
1 inch	=	25.40 mm	=	2.54 cm
¹⁄₈ yard	=	11.43 cm	=	0.11 m
¼ yard	=	22.86 cm	=	0.23 m
³⁄₈ yard	=	34.29 cm	=	0.34 m
½ yard	=	45.72 cm	=	0.46 m
⁵⁄₈ yard	=	57.15 cm	=	0.57 m
¾ yard	=	68.58 cm	=	0.69 m
⁷⁄₈ yard	=	80.00 cm	=	0.80 m
1 yard	=	91.44 cm	=	0.91 m
1¹⁄₈ yards	=	102.87 cm	=	1.03 m
1¼ yards	=	114.30 cm	=	1.14 m

Canada/U.S. Measurement				Metric Measurement
1³⁄₈ yards	=	125.73 cm	=	1.26 m
1½ yards	=	137.16 cm	=	1.37 m
1⁵⁄₈ yards	=	148.59 cm	=	1.49 m
1¾ yards	=	160.02 cm	=	1.60 m
1⁷⁄₈ yards	=	171.44 cm	=	1.71 m
2 yards	=	182.88 cm	=	1.83 m
2¹⁄₈ yards	=	194.31 cm	=	1.94 m
2¼ yards	=	205.74 cm	=	2.06 m
2³⁄₈ yards	=	217.17 cm	=	2.17 m
2½ yards	=	228.60 cm	=	2.29 m
2⁵⁄₈ yards	=	240.03 cm	=	2.40 m
2¾ yards	=	251.46 cm	=	2.51 m
2⁷⁄₈ yards	=	262.88 cm	=	2.63 m
3 yards	=	274.32 cm	=	2.74 m
3¹⁄₈ yards	=	285.75 cm	=	2.86 m
3¼ yards	=	297.18 cm	=	2.97 m
3³⁄₈ yards	=	308.61 cm	=	3.09 m
3½ yards	=	320.04 cm	=	3.20 m
3⁵⁄₈ yards	=	331.47 cm	=	3.31 m
3¾ yards	=	342.90 cm	=	3.43 m
3⁷⁄₈ yards	=	354.32 cm	=	3.54 m
4 yards	=	365.76 cm	=	3.66 m
4¹⁄₈ yards	=	377.19 cm	=	3.77 m
4¼ yards	=	388.62 cm	=	3.89 m
4³⁄₈ yards	=	400.05 cm	=	4.00 m
4½ yards	=	411.48 cm	=	4.11 m
4⁵⁄₈ yards	=	422.91 cm	=	4.23 m
4¾ yards	=	434.34 cm	=	4.34 m
4⁷⁄₈ yards	=	445.76 cm	=	4.46 m
5 yards	=	457.20 cm	=	4.57 m